A Taiwanese Immigrant's Journey to Kansas City

A Business, Music, and Community Leader

A Taiwanese Immigrant's Journey to Kansas City

A Business, Music, and Community Leader

BENNY "GOODMAN" LEE

StoryTerrace

Text Benny Lee

First print May 2025

www.StoryTerrace.com

CONTENTS

FOREWORD

Benny Lee is truly an inspiration in every aspect of his life. Long before I had the privilege of meeting him, I had heard countless stories from friends and colleagues about this remarkable business leader who had immigrated to the United States from Taiwan. When we eventually met and served as trustees on a not-for-profit board, our professional connection quickly evolved into a lasting friendship I deeply value.

Many admirable qualities define Benny, but four stand out prominently: his business acumen, philanthropic spirit, passion for music, and, above all, his unwavering devotion to his family.

Benny's business success is a testament to his relentless work ethic and perseverance. He has earned the respect and trust of employees, customers, and peers alike. He is one of the hardest-working individuals I've ever known, and he surrounds himself with capable, confident professionals who flourish under his positive and empowering leadership. It's telling that employees often say they work for "Benny" rather than naming the company—proof of the strong, respectful culture he cultivated, one that deserves to be studied and emulated.

Equally remarkable is Benny's deep commitment to philanthropy, particularly in the Greater Kansas City area.

He gives generously, supporting causes that resonate with his values and beliefs. Benny and his wife, Edith, are frequently recognized as major donors or primary sponsors of important events. Beyond financial support, Benny actively serves on numerous boards. The many honorary and emeritus titles he holds—including one from the Command and General Staff College Foundation at Fort Leavenworth—speak volumes about the impact of his contributions.

Benny's love for music is another source of inspiration. Motivated by passion, he took up the clarinet later in life and is now well known for his talent and joyful performances. While he also studied piano, it's the clarinet that truly showcases his musical heart. Many of his philanthropic efforts support music and the arts, and it's always a delight when he hosts events at his home, treating guests to live clarinet performances that create a warm and unforgettable atmosphere.

At the heart of everything Benny does is his family. He is a devoted husband to Edith—his true partner in life and business—and a proud father who beams with joy when speaking about his daughters and their accomplishments. While Benny remains modest about his own successes, he is always eager to celebrate the achievements of his loved ones. There are countless ways in which Benny's life serves as an example to others. Readers of this book will no doubt be inspired by his journey, just as I—and many others—have been.

Those fortunate enough to know Benny are consistently enriched by his wisdom, humor, humility, and generous spirit.

His ability to build bridges between the Greater Kansas City area and individuals and communities in Taiwan is just one more reason why he is so deeply admired.

Brigadier General Bryan W. Wampler
United States Army Retired
Bryan Wampler

TODAY'S SPECIAL VALUE

I checked my watch. It was nearly midnight in West Chester, Pennsylvania, home of the QVC Home Shopping Network. A network spokesperson would begin pitching my company's Steamfast steamer to a national television audience in a few minutes. QVC graciously offered to feature it as "Today's Special Value," and at least once an hour for 24 hours, they would promote it to viewers at a special low price.

Our steamer was a popular item with QVC because it was energy efficient, environmentally friendly, and, perhaps, most importantly to the network, a new product it could offer viewers at a special low price. In fact, the network already accounted for about 40 percent of total company sales. In 2002, I was excited that they had selected it for the special value promotion, in which they introduced new products. They had asked me to create a new clothes steamer for the promotion so it would be a completely original item that had never been sold before. I was grateful for their confidence in both the product and my company, and I hoped the national exposure would help boost sales.

Although I have never considered myself smarter or a better businessperson than anyone else, I already enjoyed a great deal of success. While living in my native Taiwan, my partner in South Africa and I sold thousands of Ginsu 2000 knives through television marketing, mainly in the U.S. market. I knew from experience that there were two kinds of TV sales:

- Informercials usually run for 30 to 60 minutes and are expensive to produce and purchase airtime.
- Commercials, by contrast, run only for two minutes or less, so they are much less expensive. They are especially effective when launching a new product before it becomes available through retailers. If the commercial is effective, retailers can sell four times as many products. Commercials were our most effective way to market Ginsu knives.

I had established strong relationships with engineers and manufacturers throughout Asia that helped me bring my ideas to market. Working with several leading U.S. companies opened the door for me to move my family to Kansas City and start my own business, Top Innovations.

So, with a track record of success, why was I so nervous?

QVC ordered 16,000 steamers on consignment for its promotion. Despite some negotiation on terms, they could return much of the product if it didn't sell. However, my manufacturer in China required full payment before shipping the products to the QVC warehouse. So, whether home shoppers purchased a single steamer, I had already invested several hundred thousand dollars in the promotion.

Shortly after midnight, the spokesperson, Maria Simone, came on the air to pitch the wonders of the Steamfast steamer, and the phones began to ring. As I nervously paced the floor, the show's director burst in following the first 12-minute segment.

"Mr. Lee, we already sold 3,000 steamers," the director said. "There is nothing to worry about. Go to your hotel and get some sleep."

"We may have sold 3,000," I replied, "but I still have 13,000 to go."

Within 20 hours, all 16,000 steamers were sold!

As I settled in to wait, my mind drifted back to my childhood in postwar Taiwan, my training in college and the military, my early business career, and finally, a series of events that enabled me to fulfill my lifelong dream of moving to the United States. As a result, I have been able to meet influential people in business, politics, and the arts, and I have been honored to be able to give back to my adopted home. I glanced at the television monitor where QVC was pitching my product, and customers were responding. The same question kept going through my mind:

How did an ordinary kid from Taiwan ever end up here?

Dinner at QVC President's home with QVC buyers and our sales team. Our chef was the famous Ming Tsai.

Ming Tsai signed his name on our menus.

CHAPTER 1: LIFE IN TAIWAN

I have been blessed with a wonderful family, loyal friends, a successful business career, and the honor of being able to give back to the city and nation I love and call home. As I often say, there is nothing special about me, but I have always been able to connect the dots in business. Where others may see challenges or roadblocks, I see opportunities.

I like to think of success as the three Cs—change, challenge, and chance. Looking back, all three have played important roles at various times. As I once joked, although change is good because it gives you a fresh opportunity, just don't change your wife because it's too expensive.

Of course, connecting the dots later in life's journey is much easier than at the beginning. I can see how I grew up in Taiwan, with its rich history and culture, shaped who I am today. My family, friends, teachers, and employers instilled in me a drive to be the best I could be and share any success I have achieved.

Many Americans know about Taiwan only from today's news headlines about ongoing threats from the People's Republic of China. Others know it as an economic powerhouse and strong ally of the United States. In fact, Taiwan is the ninth-largest trading partner of the United States. World travelers enjoy its rich history, impressive scenery, and friendly people. For me, it simply is home.

Despite being a relatively small nation where people just want to peacefully go about their business, other countries have tried to control and exploit Taiwan for much of its existence. From the late 13th to early 17th centuries, the Han Chinese gradually came into contact with Taiwan and started settling there. Named Formosa by Portuguese explorers, the Dutch colonized the southern part of the island in the 17th century, while the Spanish built a settlement in the north that lasted until 1642. These European settlements were followed by an influx of Hoklo and Hakka immigrants from Fujian and Guangdong across the Taiwan Strait.

In 1662, Koxinga, a loyalist of the Ming dynasty who had lost control of mainland China in 1644, defeated the Dutch and established a base of operations on the island. The Qing dynasty defeated Koxinga's descendants in 1683 and annexed their territory in Taiwan. The Qing ceded Taiwan and Penghu to the Empire of Japan after losing the first Sino-Japanese War in 1895. Taiwan enjoyed industrial growth and became a productive rice and sugar-exporting Japanese colony.

During the Second Sino-Japanese War, Taiwan served as a base for launching invasions of China, Southeast Asia, and the Pacific during World War II. More than 207,183 Taiwanese soldiers served in the military of Imperial Japan during these wars, and 30,304 of them were killed, according to Japan's Ministry of Health, Labor and Welfare. Japanese implemented imperial education in Taiwan, and many Taiwanese fought for Japan in the last years of the war. The two nations were friendly then and remain so today. After the initial conflicts, Japan made significant contributions to rebuild Taiwan, although there was some resistance fighting.

In my father's era, they made a favorable impression, especially when compared to Chiang Kai-shek's iron rule. The Taiwanese people never forgot how he used the military to oppress them. In fact, many of the people who resisted Chiang Kai-shek's oppression later became leaders in the Democratic Progressive Party that rules today.

In return, the Taiwanese people have also been generous to Japan. After a devastating earthquake hit Japan in March 2011, Taiwan's government, businesses, and private citizens came to their aid. They donated $230 million, which was as much as the combined donations from all other nations. Japan appreciated the support and always treated visitors from Taiwan well.

In 1945, following the end of hostilities in World War II and shortly before I was born, the nationalist government of the Republic of China, led by the Kuomintang, took control of Taiwan despite the United States and the United Nations saying there was no transfer of sovereignty. In 1949, after losing control of mainland China in the Chinese Civil War, the Chinese government under the KMT withdrew to Taiwan, where Chiang Kai-shek imposed martial law. The KMT ruled Taiwan as a single-party state for 40 years until democratic reforms in the 1980s. The first-ever direct presidential election was held in 1996. During the post-war period, Taiwan experienced rapid industrialization and economic growth, and it became known as one of the "our Asian Tigers" or "our Asian Dragons." In short, it took centuries of diplomacy and bloodshed for Taiwan to earn the independence it enjoys today. Although the Chiang Kai-shek period was marked by bloodshed, his son was much better. The great President Lee Teng-hui later was the key person in leading the peaceful transition of power to the Democratic Progressive Party. Although China may like to throw its weight around and try to intimidate the Taiwanese people, they have experienced far too much turmoil to easily give up their freedoms.

Looking back at the nation's past, I realize how much easier it was for my daughters to study history in the United States, whose story began in 1776. instead of thousands of years ago. However, I also understand that the Taiwanese government has significantly changed how history is taught in primary schools. It has removed much of the 4,000 years of Chinese history and focuses instead on Taiwan itself. This fact is understandable because they intend to separate Taiwan and China. Most of the kids in the Far East study hard, sometimes from 7 a.m. to 11 p.m., to catch up on homework from their intensive extra classes.

Although my personal story began when I was born during Chiang Kai-shek's authoritarian rule, my family's roots in Taiwan reach back for many generations. My grandfather, Hsing Wang Lee, came from a poor family but worked hard to provide for them, eventually becoming a businessman. He imported dye from Japan, and my father followed in his footsteps, mixing different colors to create additional products in Taiwan. My grandfather's first wife, May Chen, came from a prominent family. She was a descendant of a high official in the Qing Dynasty who ruled the Taipei Talonton area and later became a successful businessman. Unfortunately, my grandmother died when my father was only three years old, and my uncle was born to his second wife.

My father, Ko-Guan Lee, was born on August 12, 1918. He worked with my grandfather in the family business, which inspired me to get involved in import-export industries. The Japanese army recruited many Taiwanese men to fight in Southeast Asia in the latter part of World War II. Because my grandfather arranged for my father to work for the police department instead, he didn't have to go to war. This decision proved to be wise because the police were highly respected at that time, and I later heard that Taiwanese soldiers were treated poorly.

Because my father's business involved importing from Japan, he had visited the nation and learned to speak good Japanese. My brother once showed me a photo of him that had been taken in Japan. My father told me that the Japanese ruled the nation harshly at that time and treated the Taiwanese as second-class citizens. Although he may have dreamed of a career other than joining the family dye business, he had limited options during the occupation. Taiwanese were not allowed to be educated in several fields, such as politics and engineering, which is why many studied medicine and became doctors. Nevertheless, I greatly admire his integrity and how he ran his business.

Sadly, he died young, at the age of 42, when I was only 13. He and my grandfather liked discussing and often arguing about world affairs during dinner. These conversations often were fueled by heavy drinking, which may have contributed to his early death. Observing them made a big impression on me, so I tried to avoid drinking alcohol as I grew up.

My mother, Siu-Yen Huang, was born on August 20, 1923, and died in 2013. She came from a more prominent family. However, she was in an arranged marriage when she was a child, so she spent a lot of time in my father's house. Her ancestors settled in the Wanhua Taipei area, where they became successful in the lumber business. They are remembered today for starting the world-famous Longshan Temple.

The temple was built in 1738 and has survived several disasters, including a bombing raid during World War II. Residents rebuilt it after every earthquake, flood, and fire without much help from government agencies or wealthy benefactors. To this day, citizens take pride in the fact that donations from the community paid for every stone and carving. Interestingly, Longshan Temple combines the Taoist, Buddhist, and Confucian faiths, unlike most temples dedicated to a single religion. Taiwan has always been inclusive in its attitude toward religion, and Longshan Temple embodies that inclusive spirit.

Our family has long been involved in the community, a tradition I am proud to carry on today. My uncle, Huang Chi-jui, was mayor of Taipei City from 1957 until 1964. I remember my mother working on his mayoral campaign when I was young. The office of mayor was an elected position from 1957 to 1961, which was not good, because most resources were controlled by KMT, which was initially

Chian Kai-Shek's party. It became an appointed position during my uncle's second term, from 1961 to 1964. It was too bad that he died young because he may have been elected to an even higher office later when the political field became more open and then been able to promote more Taiwanese in politics.

His son, Huang Shu-Wei, followed in his political footsteps. He was elected as a member of the National Assembly (closed in 2005) and then as a member of the legislature Yuan, the most important assembly to monitor Taiwan's government. Although he became a legislator, he eventually grew tired of politics and instead focused on his family business and community service, such as being chairman of Longshan Temple.

The tradition has continued with my cousin, who currently is chairman of the temple board, which hires the president who runs the temple. My other uncle, who was extremely close to me, was chairman of the temple for a long time and made significant contributions to it before he passed away. My cousin followed him to promote it, and because he was a legislator, it was a good use of his resources.

I was close to my uncle (who was the cousin of the uncle who was mayor) and his daughters and visited their home often. He held a prestigious position as head of accounting at the Taiwan Telecommunications Bureau until he retired. My uncle was highly respected on my mother's side of the family and was the one who mediated and resolved any disputes. He also inherited a great deal of property. He considered me a close family member and was proud of me.

After he retired from the Telecommunications Bureau, he devoted his time to Longshan Temple. At that time, many homeless people stayed at the temple because it had a mission of helping the poor. However, there were no rules, and it created a bad image in the community. My uncle developed a successful plan to continue helping the homeless while keeping the temple clean and safe for worshippers. Using what we call public relations today, he encouraged the local media to report on the problem to create social pressure for change.

At the same time, he led the way in cleaning, remodeling, and modernizing the temple, which his family continues to do. Visitors to the temple today are impressed by how fresh, clean, and organized it is and its many educational programs and other social activities.

My uncle's daughter, Jasmine Huang, with whom I am also very close, was on the temple's board of directors after she retired. Jasmine was an accounting major and once worked in my office. My uncle was proud of my business success, and there are few people whose respect I value more.

My mother's family lived in an old, traditional-type house on the bank of the Tamsui River. Visitors crossed the big entrance into a square large enough to play ball before entering the main hall. Three or four generations lived in this big house, and all the families gathered in the main hall to worship during the Lunar New Year or other important occasions. Forty years ago, Japanese media reporters visited Taiwan to write a story and visit this house. They asked how so many family members could get along without fighting.

Developers have removed the old building and replaced it with a modern high-rise. The management is excellent, and many of my relatives still live there.

All my family is Buddhist, which is the dominant religion in Taiwan. The country is less than 10 percent Christian (including 5.5 percent Catholic), but I converted when I married my wife, Edith, who comes from a Christian family. Although Buddhists discourage marrying a person of a different faith, my family was open-minded and approved of our marriage. We had a Christian marriage ceremony in the church, and my mother sang the songs and celebrated with us. My father's side of the family was more open-minded, while my mother's side was conservative, and my personality combines both traits. Although I tend to be quiet and reserved by nature, I also enjoy being social with my friends (as anyone who has heard me play the clarinet would agree).

Taiwanese parents at that time arranged future marriages for their children while they still were young. Although that mostly worked out well for my parents, my mother later learned that my father had another wife and several other children. She graciously took in his other three kids after my father passed away so they would have my father's name. When my father passed away at a young age, she never remarried and became friends with his other wife. My mother had a great heart and extended her love to my father's second family. At that time, the community accepted a man having more than one wife, although only one was legally registered. For example, Yung-Ching Wang, a famous businessman who founded Taiwan Plastic and was worth $20 billion, had three wives. Although society accepted this practice at the time, he could register only one of his wives.

Every Taiwanese citizen has an identification card that shows the names of their parents, and each household has a registration book that shows the number of family members. This information is required for many things, such as buying a house or getting married. My mother accepted the other children so their identification would show my father's name instead of "unknown," which was really important for them.

Of course, I knew nothing about the drama surrounding my family and nation when I was born. My parents named me Yung Chieh Lee at birth (the American name "Benny" would come later). Every character in the Chinese language has a meaning. Yung Chieh means "forever distinguished," which sets a high standard for me to achieve.

I arrived at a turbulent time in postwar Taiwan. What came to be known as the February 28 Massacre was an anti-government uprising that the Kuomintang government of the Republic of China violently suppressed. Directed by provincial governor Chen Yi and President Chiang Kai-Shek, thousands of civilians were killed beginning on February 28, 1947. The incident is considered one of the most important events in Taiwan's modern history and influenced the Taiwan independence movement. Chiang Kai-shek ruled the nation with an iron fist and once said, " I would rather kill 99 innocent people than allow one bad person to survive." I was the third of four boys, keeping my mother busy while my father worked. An uncle, who was married to my father's sister, had no children. Before I was born, my mother had promised to give me to them to raise, but she said I was so cute that she asked him to wait for the next one. This is how my younger brother ended up as the son of my uncle, who became wealthier than our family after my father died. Changing my brother's last name to his last name was essential to continue the family tree.

My uncle (who was married to my father's sister) was strong and hardworking. His son (my younger brother) passed away earlier because of smoking. He arranged for his daughter, Jamie Chen, to study in Canada for high school and college. She loves music and has good piano skills for popular music. When she returned to Taipei, she was sometimes invited to play in public places. During my recent trip back to Taipei for a family reunion, my daughter Elizabeth, my wife Edith, and I spent time together and chatted about our family. I really enjoy times like that.

He operated a successful theater sound business, including building a theater amplifier system, and he also owned a film projection business. Because movie theaters were not as common at that time, he also had a team that set up outdoor theaters. He later opened a small indoor theater for movie industry members to use when they wanted to screen new movies. Everyone who worked in the industry or was interested in movie history at that time knew about it because it was the only one in Taipei or even Taiwan, and thousands of new movies played there. Many people still remember it today. Filmmakers working on a documentary about the movie industry recently contacted his granddaughter. They all remembered the Tai-Ying Movie Preview Room and included it in their film.

Our relationship was good because my brother became their son and carried their last name. My uncle let our family stay in his extra apartment, which was a big financial help. That apartment was close to his home and office building on Wuhan Street in Taipei. We lived on the fourth floor, and the floor below us was rented to a couple with a young girl who loved to sing. Her singing partner, Teresa Teng, became world-famous after leaving her partner in the Chocolate Sisters and studying in Japan.

Although they were together as a duet for only a short time, most people in Taiwan and China knew Teresa's songs. (You can learn more about her life and music at Teresa Teng: https://en.wikipedia.org/wiki/Teresa_Teng.

There was a saying in China: "In the daytime, we listen to old Teng (Deng Xuai Ping, the Communist leader from 1978 to 1990)." Chinese people listen to little Teng (Deng) only secretly at night. I still have an old black-and-white picture of Teresa Teng and her partner, the Chocolate Sisters, from when I invited them to our school for the student dance party. People are surprised to learn that I knew Teresa Teng when she was a teenager.

Although people in China widely admired her music, she loved Taiwan and volunteered to sing for the Taiwanese army many times because she also loved the military. Despite being famous there, Teresa never visited China; when she died at a young age, the entire nation mourned. In 2020, CNN ranked

Teresa as one of the most influential singers of the past 50 years.

My second-oldest brother ended up working in the movie and tea industries, and he later came to work for me. We were really close, but he unfortunately died in his sleep from an aneurysm at age 42. I am grateful that I was successful enough at that time to help his family financially and purchase an apartment for them when he was still alive and worked for me. His son told me that he really appreciated that gesture and that he continued living in that apartment after his mother passed away. My brother had a genuinely nice character and was good in social settings, just like our father. People who knew him called him a nice man.

Buying an apartment was much less expensive at that time, and it was in a good location on a main road. I recently met his son during a visit to Taiwan. He had joined the army and retired as a major, so he received monthly payments from his military retirement fund. He sold his father's apartment and bought two other ones so he could live in one and rent the other. He has a great attitude and remembers how I was able to help his father. Helping care for your family simply is what is expected in Taiwan, although a few people fight for estate distributions in court, which is not something a good family does. However, this situation may change in the future.

When I was in primary school from 1953 to 1959, my family lived in a two-story building on a side street in central Taipei, which was common at that time. The area where I lived as a child was called the Dadaochen district of Taipei, a prosperous business area with many small family shops and businesses.

I recently mentioned to a friend that I had lived in the city as a child. He replied that our family must have been well off because many people lived in the poor countryside and farmed. In 1969, when I worked for Bendix and shared an apartment with my friend Ray, my landlord heard I had a telephone at home. I was surprised when he said, "You are from a wealthy family if you have a phone." I never realized until then how poor the nation of Taiwan was. I have fond memories of my early childhood. One of the earliest is the green dye my father mixed in a large bowl for his business. Although he was a good father, it was a different time, and fathers had a much different role. He worked hard at his business, but I don't remember him ever helping me with my homework or taking us on family vacations. However, in the Buddhist tradition, our family always got together to celebrate the new year, which is as big of a holiday in Taiwan as Christmas is in the United States. People also take time to remember their ancestors on an April holiday that is like Memorial Day in the United States.

From movies to music to early television shows, American culture was a big influence in the postwar years. I didn't have an opportunity to see many movies, although I recall the 1960 film Exodus about the founding of the nation of Israel. U.S. soldiers were stationed in Taiwan at the time, and there was an American Officers' Club where people could go to dance. Even then, many Taiwanese dreamed of moving to the United States for economic opportunities and because of concerns about threats from the Communist government in China. That certainly was my dream from an early age, and I was fortunate enough to eventually turn it into reality.

My family was far from wealthy, but we were happy. However, everything abruptly changed when my father unexpectedly died in 1959 when he was just 42 and I was 13. Besides the emotional shock of his death, we suddenly found ourselves with no income because my mother had never worked outside the home.

My uncle, the mayor of Taipei at the time, was a godsend. Despite my mother's lack of education and work experience, he found jobs for her, first at the zoo and then with the census department. She was a patient, hardworking woman dedicated to learning. My mother also could write beautiful characters on cards as part of her job in the census department. The fact that my uncle and others helped us in our time of need made a big impression on me, which is why I have compassion for the homeless and help them whenever I can. It also may be one of the reasons why I appreciate the security of owning a lovely home are as follows: I attended primary school for six years before attending Taipei Municipal Jianguo Middle School from 1959 to 1962. I already expressed my interest in music and electronics by displaying record albums, amplifiers, and similar items at the school festival. When I was a student at the Tatung Institute, my uncle taught me at an early age to assemble a 626L push-pull amplifier, which I demonstrated during the college festival, using records by jazz musicians such as Glenn Miller and

Benny Goodman. I also took an electronics course in my junior college.

I excelled in school but consider myself an average student. However, I became interested in electronics, a burgeoning industry after the war. My uncle taught me about electronics (vacuum tubes instead of semiconductors), played his jazz records, and helped instill in me a lifelong love of music. Because he loudly played the Glenn Miller Story soundtrack and Johann St. Strauss's waltzes to test his sound system, I learned these tunes while I was still a teenager.

I was selected as chief (or president) of students for the five-year college, and George Chen was president of the university students. We assembled on the school playground every morning and spoke to all the students about what was happening that day. I spoke one morning, and George spoke the next day. This routine helped me develop leadership and public speaking skills and overcome my shyness. I was the Student Management Team president, and the school allowed us to self-manage student affairs. George went on to become president of Tatung America, lives in Dallas, and once visited me in Kansas City.

I played trombone in the school band and finished second in a competition during summer camp where a trumpet player won first place. Thanks to my uncle, I became interested in jazz and eventually built a large record collection. When our teacher asked us to select an English name, I chose "Benny" because I loved the music of big band leader Benny Goodman. (And I like to think that I am both Benny and a good man.) Although not a gifted athlete, I enjoyed playing badminton, soccer, and table tennis (ping-pong.) I am a better ping-pong player than the average American, although table tennis is not as popular here as it is in Asia. I had a table in my house at Briarcliff West in Kansas City, which had high ceilings, and we later moved it to the dining room in our office on Troost Avenue.

My uncle also found me a job in the library in 1962, which expanded my horizons and provided additional income for our family. I started out sweeping floors for a few months, probably because the president wanted to test me. He soon moved me to the editorial department, where I wrote book names on cards. This opportunity to connect with books was very helpful to me.

Although our family managed to get by, I knew that I would have to continue my education if I were to not only earn a decent living but also help my mother and siblings. My oldest brother earned excellent academic scores and entered the best high school in the city, Taipei Municipal Jianguo Middle School. Although he had an opportunity to continue his education at the university, he decided instead to take a government job in the Taipei City Symphony's administrative department. This way, he could support our family financially so my mother could afford to pay tuition for my second brother and me. My brother is an honest, hardworking person, and the government position was a good career choice for him until he retired. I later hired him as an administrator in my business to help repay him for his generous contribution to our family when I was young.

After spending two years in high school, followed by three in college. I was accepted by the Tatung Institute of Technology, which a large appliance company had founded. The founder had started a college near the company and encouraged students to work while attending classes. The books we read were copies instead of originals. Copyright laws were much more relaxed then, and most underdeveloped countries, such as Taiwan, didn't enforce them. The world community agreed that education was more important than strictly enforcing the law as written. However, Taiwan firmly enforces its copyright laws today, and violators may even face jail time.

I studied electrical engineering and again considered myself just an average student, ranking 12th out of 27 students in my class (there originally were 55 students, but several dropped out or transferred to other schools.) Although I was more interested in the emerging field of electronics, it was not a separate major then; instead, it was included in electrical engineering. However, I also learned other skills that would serve me well in life, such as public speaking and leadership.

I didn't go straight into the workforce after college because Taiwan, like Israel and several other countries, which require compulsory military service. At that time, everyone had to serve in the military. If a young man didn't serve, he might have trouble finding a wife, because people might assume something was wrong with his body or health. As a college graduate, I was qualified to become a reserve officer in the Air Force following two months of tough new-soldier training during summer breaks from school. I served in the military in 1968 and 1969.

There are several islands off the coast of Taiwan, and I was stationed on one of the many Matsu Islands called West Dog. Because we were close to the Chinese mainland, I didn't tell my mother where I was so she wouldn't worry. My brother told her I was on Penghu Island instead of West Dog. I didn't return home until I retired a year later.

Although the Cold War was heating up at the time, there was not much action on the island, and I spent much of my time shuffling paperwork. The best thing that happened to me was meeting Ray Hsiao, another reserve officer, who would become a close friend. I served as a communication officer in the battalion office, while Ray served as a communication officer for the company. Like me, Ray loved music and taught me how to play guitar and how basic chord structure worked. I learned such chords as:

C - notes 1 3 5 (in America - C E G)

Cm - 1 3b 5 (or C Eb G)

C7- 1 3 5 7b (or C E G Bb)

C6- 1 3 5 6 (or C E G A)

Cm7- 1 3b 5 7b (or C Eb G Bb)

This experience has benefited me for the rest of my life. Although including the principle is much more complicated, it was good enough for me to use. Because music is endless, you can spend your whole life learning about it by playing an instrument, not understanding scores, or even composing music.

Although things were quiet on the Matsu Islands when I served there, China had bombed another island, Kinmen, with 57,000 cannonballs in three hours, 10 years earlier on August 23, 1958. We called this the 823 Bombing in Taiwan. Our military defeated them with the help of U.S. technology, and it became known as the August 23 War. The military had used Sidewinder AIM-9 missiles to shoot down several of Communist China's airplanes. The Taiwan Air Force shot down several F86 Chinese planes. This was the first time Taiwanese pilots had fired these U.S. missiles in an actual shooting war. The Chinese Air Force wondered how the Taiwanese Air Force could shoot so well. Although the tensions had cooled in the ensuing decade, China had boasted that it was going to bomb the island again to commemorate the anniversary because the same Communist team that had bombed Kinmen Island had been moved across from our island.

On the evening of August 22, everybody was on edge. We had to collect empty bottles and fill them with water in case war came and bullets and other ammunition were distributed. My friend Ray said, "Look at our faces— we should not belong to short-life people. So, we should be OK." (This was known as physiognomy.)

Nevertheless, we were still worried. However, despite all of China's propaganda about invading our islands, the bombs never came. As my friend said, "We will not die here." By the time I completed my military obligation, I felt as if I had spent my entire life preparing, although I was not exactly sure for what. Finally, after completing my college education and military service, I was eager to launch my career. I needed to find a job.

Two months of reserve officer military training in the summer time

Working in Taipei City Library when I was 13 years old

My uncle and aunt (my father's sister)

In school I displayed the amplifier that I made using a vacuum tube.

Chocolate Sister sang at our school for a party. Teresa Teng (left) became one of most famous singers in the world.

CHAPTER 2: SETTING THE STAGE

A long career looks much different at the end than at the beginning. I now see that each position I held contributed to the experiences and connections I would need to continue moving forward. At the time, however, I walked through the doors open to me, eager to see where they might lead.

After graduation, my buddy Ray and I started a company that tried to produce something called the music box. This was a boxlike, rectangular speaker, but instead of an actual speaker inside, many colorful lights lit up when music played. These colors varied depending on the frequencies of the music being input. After selling a few music boxes to our friends, our lack of marketing knowledge kept us from selling more, so we shut down the business and looked for real jobs. However, that experience encouraged us to become entrepreneurs, although neither of us may have known what the word meant at the time.

Ray and I decided to work together and applied to the same company. Of course, we were naïve then and didn't realize it was unlikely that someone would hire not just one but two inexperienced men fresh out of the military. However, one thing we had going for us was the timing. Because of Taiwan's proximity to the vast Asian market and access to a skilled, affordable workforce, many U.S. companies expanded to Taiwan in the postwar years. RCA manufactured computers and coils, and Ampex made computer components. As it turned out, Ray found a job with RCA while I joined the car radio division of Bendix in 1969. I worked as a technician for $75 a month, which was not a bad salary then. That first job led to a succession of other positions where I could increase my pay and, just as significantly, learn valuable new skills.

From Bendix, I went to Philco-Ford, which manufactured televisions. In 1970 and 1971, I worked in the engineering department as a junior design engineer. I remember being happy with my monthly salary of NT4000, which was $100 in U.S. dollars. Of course, that was only about 10 or 20 percent of the average U.S. salary then, which was about $1,000 to $2,000 a month.

Later, in 1971, I had an opportunity to join Arvin Industries, another U.S. company that manufactured car radios. Both companies were in the Taoyuan area. I started as a quality control engineer and later became a quality assurance supervisor. One benefit of working for American companies was the opportunity to learn about such important things as operating procedures, systems, engineering drawings, and change orders, which would serve me well throughout my career.

After a few years, I accepted a position in 1972 that dramatically changed my career trajectory and ultimately led me to the United States. Midland Radio, based in Kansas City, Missouri, had set up a purchasing office in Taiwan. It was owned by Kansas City-based Western Auto and Beneficiary Co. of New York City, a top 500 U.S. business then.

These arrangements were popular with American companies because of Taiwan's successful duty-free zone near the port. I was involved with inspections inside this zone, although other inspections were done outside the duty-free zone. Workers exiting the zone were rigorously checked to ensure they did not remove any goods, and all material imported from other countries was paid no duty because it would be used only in the zone. The Kaohsiung Expert Zone was successful and became a pioneer project for similar duty-free zones. Many well-known companies set up factories in the zone, and because the system was so successful, other nations followed Taiwan's example. It was a clever way of handling exports.

I started as a shipment inspector and eventually made helpful business connections. I visited several factories and learned many things from them that I could later use when I became a businessperson and office manager. Mr. Mori, Midland's vice president of Far East engineering, interviewed me. He was a competent engineer, spoke excellent English, and understood the company well because he had worked for Midland USA for a year or two. Because Mr. Mori was Japanese, he oversaw the Midland Japan office and was the chief engineer for the Far East. He often traveled to Taiwan and other Asian countries for business. One time, I traveled to Hokkaido, Japan, in the winter when the snow was piled one to two meters high, and they had to shovel it to create a road.

He visited Taipei for a few days each month, and I always

respected him as my mentor for my job and personal matters. I remember that he enjoyed drinking beer and talking about his many travel experiences. My good friend and former boss Richard Looney and I recently discussed how we would enjoy seeing him again. He must be at least 90 by now.

Many of these factories later would approach me with new products to see if I could introduce them to Midland or Western Auto. I learned the quality control system using the Military Standard AQL chart. The most used system then was Tighten Inspection AQL 2.5, which was considered a four percent acceptable level of significant defects. Several months later, because of office politics, Midland fired the manager of the Taiwan office. John Lane, the US president of Midland, approached me with an unexpected offer.

"Do you want to become manager of the Midland Taipei office?" he asked.

"No," I replied. "I'm not qualified."

I answered honestly because I was afraid of being fired if I accepted the position, and they later found out that I lacked the qualifications. I had good reason to be concerned because they had already fired two office managers, one a local man who had retired from the military and the other an American.

I have always tried to be honest and humble, although sometimes I forget and show off too much. When you are humble, you make more friends. True humility doesn't mean showing you are weak; instead, it reveals the quality of your personality. I later discovered that in the United States, showing off is acceptable as part of inspiring and encouraging people to do good things socially. This is why so many awards are given to regular people after they do something good for the community.

Thankfully, John Lane tried to change my mind. "Benny," he said, "when you are young, it's a good opportunity to learn about management." He finally convinced me. "OK," I said. "Give me one year as acting manager so I can be ready to be the official manager."

And that is precisely what happened. I officially became manager of the small office, which employed about 10 people, including engineers, inspectors, shippers, and secretaries. Midland marketed CB radios and later changed to land mobile radios. Eventually, it also took over part of import purchasing for Western Auto, including bicycles, garden tools, fans, and lounge chairs. I became involved with purchasing its signature Western Flyer bicycles and ceiling fans, and the diverse product line led to a wide range of industry connections. I introduced Giant Bicycle Company to Western Auto, and they remain a leading worldwide brand today.

The move also turned out well for my old friend Ray. I introduced him to Teresa, who worked in the company. They got married and lived in Toronto before he passed away. She then moved back to Taiwan, and I visited her several times when I traveled to Taipei. Christina, another Taiwanese girl working in the Midland Taipei office, later left for Channel Master. She married her German colleague, Heinz, and lived in Munich. They love classical music, and Edith and I had a great time when we stayed at their home during a recent trip.

I soon met Richard Looney, the new vice president for the Far East, who remains a close friend. Richard is highly intelligent, works hard, is a quick learner, and is always well-informed. I can't say enough good things about him as a boss, mentor, and, most importantly, a friend. I am grateful that he allowed me to become an entrepreneur despite being young and relatively inexperienced.

Richard was promoted to president when the Midland president retired and moved to the Kansas City headquarters. Pat O'Sullivan took his place. Unlike Richard, he preferred working with American managers, so he transferred me to Hong Kong, where I became a marketing engineer because of my engineering background. I worked with the person overseeing international sales and traveled with him to several countries, including my first European visit in the late 1970s. Again, learning to work with people from different cultures would serve me well throughout my career. International travel opened my eyes to many things I had not experienced before. For example, in 1976, at Tivoli Gardens in Copenhagen, I saw a sign with directions to the restroom—written in Chinese. I don't know why because I saw very few Asians on the street.

I traveled to Hong Kong in 1975, my first overseas trip. During my visits, I stayed at Hyatt Regency in Tsim Sha Tsui. Because Taiwan still was under the control of Chiang Kai-shek at that time, we heard only the news that the government permitted. In Hong Kong, I saw many newspapers with different viewpoints, which opened my eyes to international affairs, especially those related to Taiwan and China. At the same time, I met several people who became long-term business associates and friends, such as S.C. Lam, an accountant, and Anna Luk, a secretary. S.C. later worked for me in Mitco's Hong Kong office, while Anna and I remained good friends.

S.C., along with another associate, William Chan, both intended to immigrate to Western countries and had a plan to move to Canada. So, after William worked in Hong Kong, I moved him to Transworld Products (now owned by Peterson Manufacturing), which I set up in 1987. He became a key person in the company and remains so today. S.C. also took care of my personal financial matters related to Taiwan, China, and the United States.

After about a year in Hong Kong, I began to miss my home country. In 1978, I accepted a position with Amerix, an Israeli company with locations in the United States, Europe, and Asia. Working for Amerix enabled me to make several good international friends, who later became business connections as well. The general manager told me a story that I have never forgotten.

"Benny, do you know how we train our kids?" he asked. "When my kid was five years old, I put him on the table and said, 'Please jump down.' He said, 'No, Father, I can't jump down because it's dangerous.' I said, 'Don't worry. I am going to catch you.' He jumped, and I didn't catch him. I told him, 'I am teaching you that you should never trust anybody, not even your father. Trust yourself.'"

Although this may have been tough love, my character is completely different than that. My wife sometimes says I trust people too quickly and easily, which has burned me a few times. I often trust people immediately before thinking about whether that trust is justified. Edith, by contrast, is more conservative and is willing to wait for people to earn her trust. However, I believe that far more people are trustworthy than untrustworthy, so there is less of a chance that I get hurt. This is another reason why Edith and I make a good team.

Although there is no such thing as 100 percent trust in business, I believe I can be trusted, even if I can't always depend on the trust of others. This is why the U.S. system of contracts is so effective. By contrast, Chinese vendors often say, "We don't need a contract because our handshake is our contract." That all depends. If you give the factory enough business, a handshake may be enough because they will not betray you and risk losing your business. However, when your business is down, they may think it is not practical to keep paying your commission, and the relationship will break. I fully understand it.

Thanks to my experience with Midland, I soon had an opportunity to fulfill a longtime dream of starting my own business. Midland closed its Taiwan office a few years after I left because of a lack of business. However, it later decided to restart the company and hire me to run it. I made them a counteroffer. "Is it possible to be your agent with a small commission?" I asked.

They agreed because they knew me and my reputation as an honest businessperson. I officially went into business for myself in July 1979. Richard Looney agreed to forward $4,000 to rent an office, furnish it, and hire a staff member, which I paid back later. Although $4,000 was not big money for Midland, it *was* a lot of money for me in Taiwan at that time.

Without the support of Richard and Midland, I am sure it would have taken me longer to start my own company.

I called my business "Mitco," which stood for Midland International Taiwan Corporation. Noel Brittain, Midland's overseas vice president at the time, joked that Mitco stood for Many Interesting Turkeys Come Over when he visited Taiwan. We became close friends when he lived in Taiwan for several years. I even invested in his brother's printing company in Las Vegas when it was short on cash, although it later went bankrupt because of poor management.

I first opened Mitco Taiwan and then a Hong Kong office in 1985. Bob McFadden, who had been chairman of Midland, left and became a consultant to the company. He introduced me to Payless Cashways around 1987, which led me to the do-it-yourself business. Payless, a building materials retailer based in Kansas City, was one of the first chains to implement a do-it-yourself strategy. It was a successful company during the 1980s and 1990s but later ran into financial difficulties.

I always make friends wherever I go. Through Payless Cashway, I got to know Jim Price's boss, Wayne Reimer, who visited the Far East with Jim and once came to my apartment for a party. He later moved from Kansas City to the East Coast. I also became good friends with his former girlfriend, M.L. Bass. I also recently met Susan Stanton, the former Playless CEO, during community events.

Jim Price, the import manager from 1978 to 1992, often traveled to Taiwan, China, and Hong Kong to source products for Payless Cashways, with my introduction. We bought many oak toilet seat covers from a factory in Taiwan.

Other major import product lines included ceiling fans, lighting, wheelbarrows, and lounge chairs. When Payless Cashways shut down its import department, Jim worked for Mitco.

Hagino San, who retired from Midland Japan as an office mechanical engineer, later worked for Mitco in Taiwan. He taught us about Japanese engineers and their hard work ethic. We learned a lot from him.

Although we had an inspector at Mitco, Edith, my wife, was also involved in bicycle inspection. Despite knowing nothing about bicycles initially, she is intelligent and a fast learner. When she went to the factory to inspect Western Auto's Western Flyer kids' bikes, she asked them to bring her a sample, which she took apart and reassembled. During this process, she found many problems. Edith is highly detailed about everything she does and uses her common sense. After a few inspections, she was able to recommend ways in which the factory could improve the product for customers. Sometimes, she is too strict because of her high standards. I know this because I am her husband, and she has had to suffer or lower her standards to be married to me.

Although Edith is not an engineer, she has good common sense. When we shipped double-stitch sewing machines, which we developed using plastic cabinets under our own name, some defective units were returned to our office. Edith learned how to repair them by consulting Ah Fu, a Taiwanese engineer. Many problems can be solved just by using common sense, plus a few techniques that she could learn quickly from either our engineer or factory engineers.

Although I was self-employed, I functioned as if I were a Midland employee. Everything was shipped directly, and they paid me a small commission each month. Eventually, we were doing nearly $50 million in annual commission business with Midland, Western Auto, and Payless Cashways, which purchased around a half-million ceiling fans. Anytime I start a new company, I think of various "what if?" scenarios. Although Midland gave me a contract in 1980 to be their agent, I thought, "What if we lose the Midland business?" This has always reminded me to never depend on just one customer and to find additional resources. At that time, I was an agent for a South African company, Tedelex. I also was an export representative for Medal Hifi (of which I was a one-quarter factory shareholder) and did general trading.

Again, my natural inclination to trust others can be both good and bad. The tradeoff of readily trusting people is that sometimes, your trust can be misplaced. On one occasion, an employee in China put my company money under his personal name. Jiang Fei, who had worked for me in my Shanghai office, was small and young. He apparently had not been trained to be honest, as was the case with several other Chinese employees. Perhaps their communist education was to blame. I also was partially to blame for giving him too much authority to do things that I didn't know about. After leaving my Shanghai office to start his own factory, he couldn't find enough business, so I hired him to start my factory to manufacture products to market in the United States.

Although he was legally in charge in China, he did not own the factory but worked for me. Because the person in charge is responsible for any legal issues in China, Jiang Fei's name was registered despite not being the owner. I didn't want my name to be there because then I would be legally responsible. However, I did give him and his engineering team 15 percent of the company's shares to encourage them. The reason I wanted to change the factory person in charge was because Jiang Fei put all the company money in a Hong Kong bank under his name. Although he did not steal the money, it was not right. I asked him to change it to the company's name in Hong Kong, but he refused. His excuse was that if we refused to pay his employees, he would go to jail. But he did not realize this was not his company.

"Well, what happens if you fire me?" he replied. "This is for my protection because if you fire me, I still have many obligations to the employees." This may have been a good reason for him but not for me because those employees worked for the factory, not him personally.

In China, if you are not careful, especially when running a factory, you could end up in jail. Things came to a head during an all-day meeting with my attorney in which we worked through lunch. If he didn't agree to change the registration to another name, we could file a lawsuit, which could take up to a year. My lawyer in China, who worked for Husch Blackwell and was introduced to me by Fan Shen, joined the negotiation. I asked to see the chops, which were used to register the company. My intention was to wait for an opportunity to take the chops. Company chops—sometimes referred to as a seal or stampù—are mandatory for doing business and take the place of the signatures that are used in Western countries. A company seal is the tangible representative and legal evidence of the company's activities abroad. The company's person-in-charge or other management personnel authorized to hold the seal are only the temporary custodians of the seal.

The chops were left on the table when we left for lunch in the factory, and my attorney said it was a good opportunity to take them and change the company registration. My Chinese attorney took the chops and left the factory. Of course, Jiang Fei was very upset when he found out after lunch—so much so that he threatened me and would not let me leave the factory. I called my attorney, who already had left with the chops. He asked me to use the speaker on my iPhone, so Jiang Fei could hear what he said: "Mr. Lee is an American citizen. If you do not allow him to leave, I am going to call the U.S. Embassy about this, and a policeman will come to rescue Mr. Lee. Then you will be in big trouble." Then he said, "Mr. Lee, please give me permission to contact the police and U.S. Embassy."

I did not say yes because I still felt I could control the situation. Jian Fei was young and stupid. If I said yes and the police came, he would be sent to jail. I didn't want to create a big problem for him or for me. I did not say yes because I was sure Jiang Fei would release me later. After 7 p.m., he took me to my hotel. Then he came to see me at the hotel and apologized for what he did. I told him that I would give him an answer. Finally, I decided to give him a lifeline, although I didn't have to do that. I took all my shares out of the factory, which I allowed him to buy back over time. I did not want to run the factory due to potential legal issues in China.

Despite the hassle, it provided a valuable lesson. Chinese companies did many things that, if not outright illegal, at least were ethically questionable. For example, they may say they shipped products even if they really did not. Or they worked with a customs broker who gets a percentage reimbursement from the government. In short, they cheat, which is why I don't want to run a company under my name. In China, if they don't like you or something goes wrong, you even could be sent to jail.

In China at that time, every parts vendor had to pay a 17 percent sales tax, which they would refund back to the factory if you were an exporter. I later heard that Jiang Fei worked with a customs broker to fake shipments and cheated the government out of its 17 percent refund. Fortunately, most of my other business ventures were much less stressful.

Although my first business was a success, not all my decisions in my personal life at that time turned out so well. I married my first wife around the time that I began working for myself, and I admit it was a mistake. I thought it would be a good match because I love music, and she taught Yamaha piano lessons, but our personalities never quite meshed. We eventually realized we just were not right for each other and got divorced, with me giving her both the house and the car. The area where we lived is now an upscale area. Although we argued a lot, and I believe we made the right decision, divorce is never smooth, and it hurt both of us emotionally.

Although my first wife was nice, her mother unfortunately tried to get involved in our lives and started making up bad stories about my mother. My mother started living with my older brother, and he took care of her after he started working for the city symphony. She worked in the police administration office, so she had her income plus a retirement fund. She retired in 1988 and lived with my older brother until I bought a new high-end apartment in 1992. However, one negative thing about living there was that we saw the protests against the prime minister who lived in our apartment building. I gave my mother NT40,000.00 (or $1,000 U.S. dollars) each month for the rest of her life, as well as a red envelope with cash for every Lunar New Year. Although this was not a small amount of money at that time, it was affordable because my business was doing well. I believe she saved a lot of money, and I loved being able to help her.

My mother was frugal and never wasted money, and she put any extra money into her bank account. Because she never had to worry about money, she could do whatever she wanted, including donating to charity in my name, because I stayed in the United States most of the time. I believe all of my relatives admired my mother because she had good sons. In 1992, I bought a 2,500-square-foot luxury apartment in one of the most famous buildings in Taipei. Many famous people lived there, including former Prime Minister Hsiao, Prime Minister Hao, and even the son of President Lee, although they later moved to newer and even better apartments. My mother stayed at that high-class apartment alone when I was in the United States until she passed away in 2013. I eventually sold that apartment for more than $2 million in 2019.

Although we were married for only a couple of unhappy years, the marriage did produce a beautiful daughter, Jenny, who lives in Los Angeles, where her mother does. She is passionate about art, and I am proud of her for graduating from California State University-Fullerton with a bachelor's degree in graphic design and illustration. I was not able to spend as much time with her as I would have liked when she was growing up because she understandably was not comfortable staying with Edith and me in Kansas City. However, she loves Los Angeles and has many friends there.

However, I am grateful that I was able to pay her tuition, tutoring, and living expenses while she was in middle school, the first few years of high school, and college. She lived with my friend in Los Angeles, and I not only paid her rent but also food and other expenses. One day I showed her a list of how much money I had spent on her, including buying her a house in Los Angeles and she understood and appreciated it. Jenny is a good girl who knows right from wrong, and we maintain a good relationship. We recently met for lunch and dinner as I was returning from a trip to Taiwan, and we enjoyed our time together. Although other demands on my time often keep me from spending as much time with my daughters as I would like, they all understand. I am sure Jenny enjoys spending time with her mother, who lives near her in the Los Angeles area.

Meanwhile, I began traveling to China, Thailand, Indonesia, and Singapore to purchase screen doors and other products. Despite the authoritarian government, I developed a love for the Chinese people, who are polite, cordial, and hardworking. In fact, at that time, they called buyers "God" because they heavily depended on them for their economic survival.

My reputation is my most valuable possession, and I guarded it closely at a time when kickbacks and bribes were not only accepted but often expected. One time, around 1987, the owner of a Taiwanese ceiling fan company came to my car and offered me about $10,000 cash in U.S. dollars, which was big money at that time. My principle was that I wanted to remain clean for Payless Cashways—as well as all my other clients—and never do anything even remotely unethical.

I was in the commission business, meaning that I was paid by Payless Cashways instead of by vendors. I told her, "You can pay me after we have no business in the future as appreciation." I thought that was a nice way to refuse and allow her to save face. Of course, she never contacted me again after we stopped doing business with Payless Cashways, and I did not expect her to pay me.

In the early days, around 1980, bribing the government, police, or tax collectors was part of doing business. Fortunately, my business, exporting, was straightforward and good for the nation, and there was no place to hide money. When I set up a buying office in China, no taxes were involved. When I invested in the steamer factory NVision, I set up my company in Hong Kong and hired Jiang Fei as my representative in China. As a result, I had no risk because you never know what the Chinese government could do to you, and you could be sent to jail if you were not careful.

The Taiwanese have a custom of giving each other red envelopes filled with cash when someone gets married. Although I gave red envelope money to my friends and relatives when they got married and could have expected them to do the same for me, my business was doing well, and I didn't want to expect anything in return. When I got married, several suppliers saw it as an opportunity to give me money in a way that seemed to be both legal and ethical, but I refused. Although accepting money may not have been wrong, I wanted to avoid even the appearance of being dishonest. A few years later, as Taiwan became more open, kickbacks and under-the-table payments became unacceptable for both legal and ethical reasons.

Edith and I closely follow political developments in Taiwan, and a new scandal is unfolding as I write my memoirs. First, I need to provide a bit of background. The nation traditionally had two political parties: Kuomintang, or KMT, which was established a long time ago under Chiang Kai-shek and the Democratic Progressive Party, or DPP. About 10 years ago, Ko Wen-Je, a doctor, founded the Taiwan People's Party, or TPP. The party began with good intentions of representing low-income and working-class citizens, especially those who needed help purchasing a house. Unfortunately, he himself became caught up by the lure of big money in politics. He was put in jail, where he may remain for the rest of his life. It was a stupid act on his part for someone who had a good education and a good job.

Ko Wen-Je ran for president of Taiwan in 2023 and lost, which turned out to be fortunate for the nation. Although he had declared his net worth to be $500,000 plus some real estate, his wife was looking at an apartment that cost $4 million. It came out later that he already owned that apartment, was looking for more, and was funneling political donations into his personal account. As it turned out, he had been accepting bribes from a real estate developer in exchange for favorable deals. He ended up being involved in as many as five scandals, including hiding a large amount of cash in a cabinet in his home.

I was surprised by the fraud that Elon Musk and his team uncovered in the U.S. federal government. I always thought the United States had a good system and that everything was black and white. There allegedly was $100 billion in Social Security paid without knowing where it went and $50 billion in fraud. Where did the money go? If the allegations are true, then our country is in trouble.

I cannot understand why people do things like that, especially when what he did was so obvious. As a doctor, he was already wealthy, so it makes no sense to accept money under the table and risk imprisonment. This scandal made me think of the time when I was young and worked in the library, and the library president encouraged me to become a lawyer or politician when I grew up. Thankfully, I took a different path through life and never wavered from my commitment to complete honesty in both business and my personal life.

As my reputation for honesty and dependability grew, I added more clients through word of mouth. Even though I was an agent for Midland in 1980, I also became a buying agent for Tedelex, a wholesaler in South Africa. They had a factory and assembled products for Sony in South Africa. Then as now, I intentionally plan for a potential crisis. Even though I had the Midland business, I never wanted to depend on one source for everything. I enjoyed visiting them in 1980, despite the country still operating under an apartheid political system. I visited Table Mountain and Cape Point in Cape Town, where the Atlantic and Pacific Oceans meet. I still remember that each had a different color.

I joined with a friend who opened a manufacturing company called Medal Electronics. We had four shareholders—Mr. Chen, who was in charge; C.K. Lee; another person; and me. C.K. worked for the electronics importer BroadMore. He is well-educated, and his father was Li Mei-Shu, a famous Taiwanese painter during the time of the Japanese occupation. C.K. later retired to promote his father's paintings and establish the Li Mei-Shu Memorial Gallery, which remains well-known in Taiwan. (Learn more at Li Mei-shu Memorial Gallery - Wikipedia.) Medal first made pocket radios but later contracted with a Japanese trading company to develop a series of low-fi components, such as tuners, equalizers, and amplifiers.

Medal sold this line mainly to a Japanese trading company, exclusively for South America, at a price of $90 freight on board (FOB) for three pieces. On behalf of Mitco, I offered him $100 for the same products, but as part of the offer, I would have exclusive rights for every buyer outside South America. We set our selling price, and for every offer above that price, I would divide the extra profit with the manufacturer. This worked well because I didn't take all of the profit if I could sell higher for a specific area.

This gave me a great opportunity to go into the market as a manufacturer and offer our own exclusive product. Also, I was not selling me-too products for which every buyer could cut out the middleman and go directly to the factory. Through this deal, I had opportunities to work with buyers around the world. When I went into business, I asked myself, "What is my specialty?" I wanted to be different either in products or price instead of selling the same items as my competitors.

Because I didn't want to depend on a single source of business, I created several channels, including:

- I was doing exclusive sales for Medal Hifi.
- I was an agent for Tedelex,
- I added Transworld Products USA in 1987 and Ginsu knives in 1998. Harry Rosenblatt introduced me to Rael Marcus, and I helped Rael get the Ginsu TV license. I was a lighting agent for Access Lighting, Singer sewing machines, QVC, and Rival. I also sold the Steam Cleaner to Candy (Europe), that company that owns Hoover. After I moved to the United States, I invested in DuraComm.

Harry Rosenblatt, my South African friend I met in 1980 who used to work for Tedelex, later started a business in Los Angeles and used me to source materials in the Far East. He had previously visited me in Kansas City when I was involved in Transworld Products, which was my first U.S. company, in 1987. He is a very smart Jewish businessman who can see the opportunities for any business. Harry started a lighting company and hired us as an agent for sourcing and inspection. After Mitco served as his buying agent for many years, in 2007 he asked if he could set up his own buying office and hire our engineer, Hugh. I told him that would not be a problem because it would save him money and give him more control. After all, he had already given me business for more than a decade, so I helped him start his Hong Kong office.

I believe this revealed my character, much like the time when Midland opened its own office in Taiwan after I had opened Mito and was their agent. After I worked as a Midland agent for a few years, one of my employees, whom I believe was jealous of my success, contributed to Midland's Taiwan office and discontinued my agency. However, I keep good relations with Midland. Harry's company remains successful today and has a large warehouse in Orange County, Calif. I recently met him for lunch on my way home from Taiwan and told him how much I appreciated him.

Through Western Auto, I met Walt Kopala, a very smart man with knowledge about a broad range of products, including hand tools. He intended to start his own business, so he helped me start Transworld, with me as the major stockholder. We set up Transworld Products in 1987 as a service company for large U.S. businesses' direct-import programs. Scott Huntress, a smart and visionary young man, was an original Transworld employee before I sold it in 1992.

He joined the company shortly after graduating from university when we had only six or eight people on staff. He loved the company and learned a great deal from Walt. He appreciated being able to work directly with me as the owner, which is not common in many companies. He sent a letter of appreciation that I still have today. We recently reconnected after more than 20 years, and I was pleased to learn that he is a successful businessman who frequently travels to the Far East and is married to a beautiful, smart woman from Shanghai.

Harry Rosenblatt introduced me to Pat Hagerty. Pat was close friends with John Flaherty, the former head of Hamilton Beach who later became president of Singer. Pat encouraged John to add a small appliance line, and we decided to start a Singer appliance division and source or develop the products in the Far East. We enjoyed great success with several products.

My first successful product for Singer in 1992 was the Juice Extractor, although another high-quality and more expensive juicer was being marketed through 30- or 60-minute television infomercials. Although that company was making a good profit, it was pricing the juicers at several hundred dollars so it could afford to pay for television time. Our approach was to create a new market for consumers who did not want to spend that much on a juicer. We found a source in China, Hop Hsing, to manufacture our juicers, and were able to purchase them for $14.50. Singer sold its Juice Giant for three payments of $33, compared to three payments of $66 for the rival Juiceman.

Most Juiceman juicers were sold through television advertising. Infomercials, which were shown on special channels, were expensive and lasted for 45 to 60 minutes. (The Singer juicer infomercial can be seen at https://www.youtube.com/watch?v=3bkx0UvUi4Q.) Because commercials are shorter—about two minutes—they also are less expensive. Although television is costly, it is a great way to raise consumer awareness. If a product were successful on television, we would introduce it to retailers. Because television had raised awareness among consumers, retailers liked to purchase them, usually at a lower price, and generally sold four times more products than television commercials did. The juicers became so popular that we chartered air freight from China to the United States for Singer. It became an amazing part of my business.

I traveled to China many times to source and develop products for Singer. One of the largest manufacturers of irons had been in Taiwan before opening another big factory in China. We asked this factory to develop a special low-priced iron that we could purchase for perhaps $5, and Singer could sell for $20 or $30. We were the first company in the world to ask the factory to develop this line of low-cost irons. Pat Hagerty had the idea of selling them at such a low price, and Tsann Kuen worked with us to design a low-priced iron that we could sell exclusively under the Singer brand name. Tsann Kuen eventually became a big appliance brand name in Taiwan and China and went public. It had its own strategy and later developed its own brand and moved production to China.

Because the Chinese economy was not completely open at that time, the RMB was not available for foreigners, so we needed to use the special foreign exchange bill. When we visited their factory in China, we stayed at a government hotel where Lee Kuan Yew, the prime minister of Singapore, recently had stayed.

Many workers came from inland China to coastal provinces to find good jobs. When they were unemployed, some would sit on the streets waiting for work and stare at you with no reaction. Once, when Pat and I arrived in Shenzhen at night, we traveled a few hours by taxi to visit the Hop Hsing Juice Extractor factory in Shunde Guangdong. Because the government was in the process of building new highways, the road we traveled on was in poor condition. Another time, when we stayed at a local hotel in a small city, we were startled to see a rat running across the ceiling. When I first began traveling in China, there seemed to be construction everywhere. Whatever other flaws China may have, they do an amazing job with their roads and other infrastructure.

Of course, we all understand now that China spent too much money to construct things that sometimes are not practical. Every city was trying to show off and invest in numerous construction projects before they had done the proper studies to demonstrate it would work. Now, we can see that China has built one of the largest high-speed trains in the world. Today, I saw the news that China, in the last 15 years, has built 40,000 km of high-speed train rails with 2,500 stations and spent more than 6.13 trillion RMB. In fact, they have overbuilt without considering the economic results.

Many stations are not being used, and they cannot even pay to maintain the high-speed train, especially now when their economy is in bad shape. However, this is the Chinese mentality—they want to show they are number one.

Although they were friendly and worked hard, the Chinese people rarely smiled, perhaps because their lives were so mundane. This began to change as the government slowly opened its economy, and more Western companies operated factories there because of the inexpensive labor. They found they could hire 10 or 20 Chinese workers for the same cost as a single worker in the West. Because of the language barrier, these companies often hired businesspeople from Taiwan or Hong Kong as middlemen. Taiwanese companies, which have a great management system, have contributed significantly to the growth of China. Six of the top 10 and 31 of the top 100 export companies are Taiwanese. One contributing factor is that many companies moved out of China because of policy problems. Many companies, especially those involved in high-tech industries, later returned to Taiwan.

I also learned about some potential pitfalls of doing business in China. In 1995, I worked with Payless Cashways to purchase an entire shipload of drywall. When the ship was ready to sail, Edith and I attended the inspection. The captain told us to come up on the boat to see our product. When we came back down, however, the local police were there to greet us.

"You are under arrest, they said. You have no right to go on the ship." They may have thought we were trying to leave the country illegally.

They took us to the police station. Fortunately, an influential agent whom we worked with in China was with us. We filled out the necessary paperwork, and I told the police, "Hey, we are doing this as a favor to China. This is a shipment to the United States, and it's bringing business to China." The police also complained about Taiwanese President Lee, who was giving a speech at Cornell University in the United States at the time. Although I didn't agree with their complaints, I was wise enough not to argue with the police. We were able to resolve the situation, and as they say, all is well that ends well.

We also enjoyed a great deal of success with the Handy Stitch by Singer. One day, I found a small, handheld sewing machine lying on the desk of our businessperson, Jean Liu. When I asked what it was, she replied that a factory we worked with had developed it. I immediately sent that sample to Singer. They loved it and placed their first order for 10,000 pieces. The orders kept coming in even before we finished shipping the first order, and we eventually had three factories manufacturing six million pieces for Singer. We were able to manufacture them for $7 or $8, and Singer sold them on television for $49.95.

Jecar engineer Ah Fu, with my guidance. developed a low-cost sewing machine called Tiny Tailor that we sold to Singer. This product was another great success, and we sold more than one million pieces. Because of the demand, we had the Sun Ngai factory make another version of Tiny Tailor. Later, I asked Ah Fu to develop a double-stitch sewing machine with a plastic cabinet, which was highly challenging. Although we finally developed this product, it was not as successful because Singer didn't purchase it.

Plastic is not as precise a material as metal and tolerance is larger, which can create problems in making it work well. A Singer engineer, Don Ringstrom, explained that a sewing machine is as complicated as a precision watch and a motor. Every time the needle comes down, it hooks another stitch. Our sewing machine, Tiny Tailor, uses a single stitch, and the thread can be pulled out. A traditional sewing machine uses double stitches. We tried to use plastic cabinets to make a double-stitch sewing machine, which was very hard. The key is using a plastic cabinet instead of the traditional iron steel casing. Although plastic substantially reduces the cost, it is very difficult to manufacture.

We faced a lot of challenges to solve the problem. It was an expensive process and, although Singer later decided not to purchase it, we did sell it under our own name. Jecar was one of the first factories to manufacture Handy Stitch. Through Jecar, I met a smart engineer named Ah Fu, who later developed many products for me after he left and started his own company when Jecar went bankrupt. It became an exclusive manufacturer for us.

One of the factories, Airtek, was one of our manufacturers to produce Handy Stitch and was a new factory when I gave them the Handy Stitch order. They secretly developed another Handy Stitch with a different outlook, which they secretly offered to Singer to compete with me. Despite my exclusive contract, one day, they cut me out of the business so they could work directly with Singer.

"Benny," the factory representative said, "Singer told me they want to do business with me directly." I later found out they already had been working with Singer by this time.

He came to my home wanting to resolve the problem, and I showed him the contract. Once again, I was thankful that Edith had a good filing system, so I was able to quickly find that simple one-page, exclusive contract. I am not sure how legally binding it was, but he agreed to give me five percent of everything he shipped for the next three or four years until our Singer business slowed down, and I was happy with the decision.

This arrangement was made through Don Ringstrom, who visited the Airtek factory to see the production of the orders. In fact, I had placed the first order with their new factory, and they kept busy filling our orders. Nevertheless, they secretly developed another product like Handy Stitch. Several years ago, I chatted online with Don after he had retired, and he said he had not realized our situation. Of course, business is business, and I couldn't complain about him personally. Although loyalty can be in short supply at times in the business world, I understood. Several years later, I ran into the factory's manager at a trade show in China. He told his people, "I want you to know that Mr. Benny Lee was our biggest buyer, and we are here today because of him." Because the Handy Stitch was just one of many products that we developed for Singer, and the others were manufactured at different factories, it really didn't hurt our business too much.

In 1987, I started Transworld Products with Walt Kopala, who had worked for Western Auto. At about the same time, I also invested in a new company called TopLan. Novell owned 95 percent of the local area network or LAN business at that time. A friend who worked in research in Taiwan knew the LAN business very well and wanted to start a company, so I invested in it. At the same time, I set up TopLan in the United States. When Walt joined Transworld Products, I offered 25 percent of both the company's shares and those of Top Innovations. I loaned him the money for his percentage of the company, and he would pay me back from his income. The network was developed by Grand Computer in Taiwan, and I set up the company in the Transworld office.

I later sold my shares in Grand Computer in Taiwan. I felt the owner was not transparent enough, and I didn't contribute much. We did make money in our first year. The key person in charge would not feel comfortable when I earned a profit from shares without contributing too much, although I did invest money to become a shareholder. I knew this relationship would not last long. When I started Transworld Product, I also registered the company TopNet Corp. and tried to promote local networks in the United States, with Michael Carr as the person in charge. However, this business was not successful.

Because there was no network standard, it was a difficult business. Each time a new version of software such as VisiCalc (an old software like Excel) loaded, the network didn't work, so our engineer had to develop a new version that accommodated the new software. Plus, a free local network would be included when Microsoft introduced Windows in 1995, which meant I could not be successful in that business.

When I moved to the United States several years later, we shut down Top Lan and changed the company name to Top Innovations. At that time, "innovation" was a modern-sounding name that indicated we were visionary.

The transition to personal computers was exciting. One day, Jay Chen, an engineer friend whom I knew from Philco Ford, said, "Benny, what are you doing now?" Jay was a testing engineer in charge of maintaining all test equipment at the Philco Ford factory. I told him I had bought a Technics organ with automatic accompaniment, which made music more fun. This was an early stage of accompaniment on the organ or keyboard. I tried to learn piano for a month but didn't continue, and then I heard a girl playing organ in a shop. It was inspiring, so I bought an organ and tried to learn to play at home. I told the story to Jay.

The important feature of the Technics organ was that when you played chords with your left hand (which I had learned from Ray in the military) and just one note of a solo with your right hand; the finger chords on the left hand were added on to the right hand. This produces the same effect as playing five fingers with your right hand, which makes the sound much richer. Of course, this feature is readily available with today's simple keyboards. I got a lot of pleasure from playing music on this organ, although I probably didn't do it the right way and used shortcuts.

Although I still enjoy playing this type of organ, I admit I have not made a lot of progress as an organist, but I nevertheless enjoy it and still use this feature on my new keyboard. For example, I have sheet music with chords for a song called "Moonlight Serenade." I included many complicated chords, not just C, F, and G. The sound effects that come out of the organ are amazing and very professional. Even today, I enjoy playing this tune to impress my guests.

At that time, nobody used a computer for small business. Sales departments had no communications software like mine, which I developed in the dBASE II 16-bit command-driven program. Most large companies used big or minicomputers, which were so expensive that most small companies couldn't afford them. You had to know the computer language and hire a special person who knew the language to maintain it.

Jay said I should learn a high-level computer language, which is easier. The syntax, dBase 2, is just like English and is command-driven. Because you had to learn the language, I used PFS first, which was simpler. After I learned PFS in a week, I trained my people and started using it in my company. PC use was inexpensive at that time because there were no copyrights in Taiwan, and people could make shipping reports in PFS. I trained my people within a month, and everyone used it to show shipping and order reports by the vendor.

Jay told me, "If you know how to use dBase II, you will not be ordinary. You will be good." I bought a book about dBase II but was scared to touch it. However, one evening when I was really bored. I started reading that book and kept reading until midnight. Then, within the first month, I read it day and night because I found it so enjoyable. I started teaching it to my people. Whatever I learn, I teach. If you can't explain something well enough to teach other people, then you really don't understand it.

Because it was a high-level language instead of machine code, my employees learned it quickly. For example, if you want to print a shipping report for one vendor or customer, you can type Use PCISHIP Index Vendor. "Use" means "Go find that file," and PCISHIP is the file name you created for a Payless customer. You ask the computer to use the vendor as an index so it will print all shipments by the vendor sequence. Within the first month, my people could use it and apply it to the shipping report, which was very important.

I understood that the ultimate method is menu-driven, so the user does not need to learn computer language software; they just follow the menu and select what they want. I hired Jennifer Huang, a computer software engineer, to join our company. I asked her to use DBII language to write software because I didn't know how to use low-level software such as Fortran (low-level is more like machine code, and higher level is more like English). Within six months, we had increased the features of the DBII-driven menu.

I also serviced Payless Cashways at that time, buying ceiling fans and lighting. I told the lighting company, "You have so many SKUs that you should use a computer." I had Jennifer write software for them using dBase II. However, my business was growing so fast that I didn't have time to start another venture. Otherwise, I would have gone into the computer business.

After we successfully developed software for our daily communications program, we offered it to Payless Cashway.

Jim Price, the import manager, worked closely with me. At the time, everyone used a Telex or fax machine for daily communication, which made it hard to find the long project history of a project, company or vendors who worked with us. At first, we cut the paper and glued that portion to group together the same subject or vendor.

Daily communication using the program we developed was much more advanced. I sent Payless Cashways the program and a modem. (Of course, they had invested millions of dollars in computer hardware and software, but they didn't have the software as I did.) Each day, we connected and sent our daily communication files by modem. The program would create a file and show who should respond to each topic (these were the days before email). Many concepts for the program were mine because Jennifer didn't understand business well enough. However, she was able to convert my business ideas into an effective program.

Although this was a perfect program that every company should use, unfortunately, I was too busy with my other business to promote it. However, that program really improved our efficiency. I sometimes thought that if I had started a software company at that time, I would still be involved in the high-tech industry. Who knows, it may have been successful because there were so many opportunities at that time.

In 1995, when traveling from Kansas City to Taipei, I sat next to the CEO of Boss Speakers. He told me he had just read about the Taipei weather online and then talked to me about email communication. As soon as we landed, I contacted my tech consultant to ask about email because, like most people, I had no idea about the internet at that time. He said Taiwan had just started with a few users as a test. I immediately signed off on the new technology, and we started using email for all our offices, which included Taipei, Taichung, Hong Kong, and Kansas City. This immediately improved efficiency and saved me a lot of money.

Hindsight is always 20/20, but I believe if I had made the right moves then, I could have built a company to rival Alibaba. I visited a several factories in China that introduced new products every year, so I always had firsthand information about product trends. If I had taken this information, especially the new products in development at the just-in-idea stage, and connected with consumers in the United States, I likely would have been really successful.

I knew immediately that the internet would be a game-changer, but with so many other ventures on my plate, I didn't have the time or resources to pursue it. Of course, other than Steve Jobs and Bill Gates, every other entrepreneur could say exactly the same thing. I had the opportunity as a shareholder in Grand Computer, and we had many former staff in the industry after they had left the company.

When I came to the United States, I read a book about the internet titled *Internet Complete Reference* by Harley Hall and Rick Stout. I still remember the first sentence: "*The internet is by far the greatest and most significant achievement in the history of mankind. It is more impressive than the pyramids and more beautiful than Michelangelo's David and more important to mankind than the wondrous inventions of the Industrial Revolution.*"

I sometimes wish that I had the knowledge and time to pursue the possibilities of the internet when it first began. One thing Edith and I both have is a good sense of logic. We use logic to run our business, which sometimes is good and sometimes I need to be vague. If we are too straightforward, I would create many enemies in the company. In the U.S. culture, when people make mistakes, we always like to find out who and why. The reason is not to punish people but to let them know they made a mistake so they would know the reason and could avoid making it again. But the problem in the U.S. culture is that we should not point out the mistakes of our employees openly, or some would even try to hide the mistakes. Our point is if they do not admit their mistake, how can they correct it in the future? So, we just need to work in a balanced way, not to complain too much but let them know in a nice way.

But as Edith says, "Don't be greedy." I always say I should have done this or that, or I could have been a billionaire if I had only taken advantage of the opportunities. But there are only so many hours in the day, and I was spread thin with my various business ventures. Instead of focusing on regrets, I would much rather be grateful for the things I have been able to accomplish. Although I had an idea for a business like Alibaba, I am content with what I have achieved with my limited education and abilities. I am fortunate to have what I have today. Although I am not superb, I should be above average.

By this time, I felt I had hit my stride as a businessman. My many ventures were flourishing, new opportunities continued to arise, and Taiwan was an attractive place to do business. We had a saying at that time: "If a sign was hanging in Taipei and it fell down, 90 percent of the people it hit would be businessmen." I also had married Edith, who worked in my company. This time, I made a wise choice, and she has been the ideal wife and mother to our children. She is a good helper in my business, stays calm, and thinks things through. I often rush in without thinking too much, which has caused me to get burned a few times.

Edith's father was a colonel in the military. With his talent and experience, he should have been a general, but as in many careers, that require having the right political connections. I believe he was more of an introvert than an extrovert, so he didn't like using connections to get promotions. He retired as a colonel, although his cousin was in a much higher position before he moved to Taipei. He even visited the United States for a few months for training at the Aberdeen Proving Ground in Maryland. He wisely purchased land in Taipei that has turned out to be valuable today. Edith said that she once thought she could never marry a Taiwanese man—but that was before she met me when she went to work for my company.

Edith's mother was from a nice, well-educated family. She studied in medical school to be a doctor. Unfortunately, before she graduated, due to the conditions in China, her family moved to Taiwan, so she did not graduate from medical school. She graduated from nursing school with high scores and was a school flower or beauty queen. After moving to Taiwan, she was a nurse in a hospital before moving to Taipei. Although it is difficult to become wealthy as a soldier, I consider her family to be upper middle class. Her uncle was mayor of a large city in China, Pingxiang Xian County Magistrate. Unlike Edith's father, he had many political connections before and after he moved to Taipei with the Chiang Kai-shek group. His son, who is Edith's cousin, worked as a flight attendant for China Airlines, which was a prestigious job. He later was elected as a legislator representing the airline's interests and now lives in Los Angeles after retiring.

When Edith started her job, she had no idea about business. She was a straightforward person, but sometimes, in business, you must be flexible. She told me I complained to her by saying, "Do not be a messenger. You need to think when I give you a message for the factory. You need to use a logical way to communicate with them and get the answer. Do not just pass my message along as only a messenger."

She remembered that comment ever since and sometimes even brings it up to me in our daily life. I coined a phrase specifically for that situation: "Don't be a transceiver and receiver. You need to pass the message with logical words." She added a lot to my business, especially in organization, which had been her major in school.

In short, I had everything I dreamed of right there in Taiwan. Well almost everything. Although I was comfortable in Taiwan, I knew it was now or never to pursue my lifelong dream of moving to the United States. I have admired the nation for as long as I can remember. Many people don't realize how many nations around the world live in freedom today because of the United States. Plus, the future of Taiwan was uncertain because of constant threats from Communist China.

It was time to embark on the adventure of a lifetime.

My first job at Bendix, working as a technician in the Engineering Department on a car radio.

Judy Hsieh - Our key secretary at Mitco Taiwan, showing Medal Mid-Fi Audio components

CHAPTER 3: KANSAS CITY, HERE I COME

Millions of immigrants arriving by ship from Europe in the early 20th century crowded the decks to catch their first glimpse of the Statue of Liberty in New York Harbor. Then, as now, it promised freedom and opportunity to anyone willing to work hard, play by the rules, give back to their new nation, and enjoy all it had to offer.

I love Taiwan and am grateful that I grew up where and when I did. I would not be who I am today without the countless family members, teachers, clients, and coworkers who encouraged me. However, like those immigrants of long ago, I always believed my destiny would someday take me to the United States.

When many Asian immigrants dream of the United States, they think of large West Coast cities such as Los Angeles, San Francisco, or Seattle. Or perhaps they consider well-known East Coast cities such as New York City or Boston. However, I found my American dream right in the middle of the country in Kansas City, which is 7,500 miles from Taipei.

I didn't learn about Kansas City from geography class but from clients such as Midland Electronics, Western Auto, and Payless Cashways, which were all based here. People not familiar with the city may be surprised to learn that it is a beautiful area of gently rolling hills, tree-lined streets, and upscale neighborhoods, with a rich arts and cultural scene and genuinely friendly people who welcome newcomers.

Of course, I didn't fully appreciate this beauty during my first visit in 1974. I stayed at the Westin Crown Center Hotel near the Hallmark Cards headquarters in the dead of winter and found the city covered in snow, which we never have in Taiwan. But the people, even strangers, were warm and made me feel at home.

People from other nations tend to form their impressions of the United States from what they see in movies and television programs. Because racial discrimination often is in the news, it is easy to assume that it is the norm. People have asked if others have discriminated against me in the United States. "Yes, I say, but in a good way. Because I have a different background and life experiences, they give me favors and want me to add a new perspective to their organizations." For example, if I were not a minority, how could I have become a board member of such prestigious organizations as the Greater Kansas City Chamber of Commerce, United Way, Command and General Staff College Foundation, Asian American Chamber of Commerce, Park University, and so many others?

The best way to make friends is to be friendly, as Confucius said in The Analects, 1992, "What you do not want done to yourself, do not do to others." I am happy now that I have more friends in Kansas City than in Taiwan. I treat them how I would like to be treated, and they welcome me with open arms. I always make it a point to try to give more than I receive from my friends.

One of the biggest challenges before immigrating was telling my employees in Taiwan. "Benny, are you leaving us?" one asked. "No, I replied. This has always been my goal." Although I turned my company over to my relatives, I continue close business contacts with them. I travel back to Taiwan at least two or three times a year, except during the pandemic. My United Airlines mileage card shows that I have traveled almost 2.5 million miles since they started keeping track in 1990, and this doesn't include flights on other airlines. I enjoy traveling for both business and pleasure, and I also traveled to Europe frequently when I had an office in Spain.

Although uprooting my family and business to move halfway around the world may seem daunting, the process went much smoother than expected. It certainly helped to have several trusted friends and business associates in Kansas City who could help me acclimate. It also helped that the move was gradual rather than abrupt. Because I was dividing my time between Mitco, my business in Taiwan, and my business interests in the United States, I would stay in Kansas City for several months and then return to Taiwan.

This was before 1995, which is why our daughter, Elizabeth, was born in Kansas City with help from Walt Kapala. At that time, we lived in a hotel near Transworld Products on Shawnee Mission Parkway near Interstate 35 on the Kansas side of the state line. Walt lived in a lovely house on 135th Street, which had been developed in 1990 and that he had purchased a few years after we started Transworld.

Edith and I remained in Kansas City for three or four months when our older daughter, Elizabeth, was born at

Shawnee Mission Medical Center (now AdventHealth Shawnee Mission). Then, we returned to Taiwan so my mother could help care for her. Our second daughter, Katherine, was born three years later. I wanted my daughters to understand Taiwanese culture and language, make some friends in Taiwan, and have a close relationship with my mother. Elizabeth and Katherine attended kindergarten in Taipei and made a few good friends. Each time they return to Taipei, they enjoy seeing those friends, especially Elizabeth. She expressed a strong interest in Spanish as a kid, and our Filipino maid tutored her. She studied Spanish literature when she attended Connecticut College.

We hired a maid to take care of Katherine. This arrangement was quite common among businesspeople in Taipei, especially if both the husband and wife worked in the business, as Edith and I did. We also had a driver, which was convenient because it was difficult to park in the city even then. Although we lived in a high-class apartment and life was good, that was not our goal.

My mother also helped, but we wanted her to enjoy her senior years. We later legally brought our maid to Kansas City to care for our daughters when they were young. She appreciates all we have done for her so that she can live in the United States. Thanks to the help of attorney Roger Hiatt, our E-2 visa allowed me to bring my family, and our maid was part of our family.

During this time, I became involved in a profitable venture marketing Ginsu knives in 1998. Most people remember the commercials for these knives, which seemed to be on television constantly during the 1970s. Sales were so successful that the manufacturer lost its focus, expanded too rapidly into other products, and went bankrupt. Rael Marcus, a friend in South Africa, approached me and said, "Benny, I know the Ginsu knife is very successful, and I want to develop it."

My friend Charlie ran a large shoe factory, and I paid a five percent royalty to use the Ginsu name for television only after he had purchased the rights from a bankruptcy court. We arranged to produce the Ginsu 2000 knife in Taiwan. It featured a serrated blade that didn't need to be sharpened and carried a lifetime guarantee, so it became a successful product for us.

My friend Rod Cox still thinks of Ginsu knives when he thinks of me. *"I always enjoyed introducing Benny to others by not only mentioning his business success but also by mentioning that he developed Ginsu knives and marketed them with his partner," he said. "Most everyone knows of the Ginsu knife and always enjoyed meeting the man who was part of that phenomenon. Not sure Benny ever wanted that to be the topic of the conversation."*

At the same time, I was still working for Singer in Taiwan. Looking back, I was walking a tightrope with my businesses, with one foot in Asia and one in the United States. However, in 1995, I reached a point where we could officially move to Kansas City full-time and adjust to American customs, some of which seemed strange to me.

Each day, another credit card company seemed eager to lend us money—at 15 percent or 20 percent interest. We still don't understand why people borrow money at such high interest rates because we always pay in full as soon as we get the bill, just as most of my friends in Taiwan did. I had never heard that borrowing money from a credit card company was a norm until I came to the United States, but unfortunately, it has become common in Taiwan and China as well. I still can't understand why people borrow spending money at such high interest rates.

Overall, however, life in the United States proved to be all I hoped it would be and more. I enjoyed many aspects of it that many Americans often took for granted. For example, I learned that Donald Hall Jr., the chairman of Hallmark Cards, drove a Honda. Don't get me wrong—Hondas are fine cars, but I expected influential business leaders to drive something more luxurious. He visited my office at DuraComm once when we were importing LED lighting. Of course, he could drive any car he wanted with his power and money. His family has contributed significantly to the Kansas City community. I even played clarinet in his home when he held a fundraiser for the Kansas City Jazz Orchestra, and I was the chair. Don and I knew each other well because of my community work. He was a key contributor to the KC Jazz Orchestra. He recommended that I join the board, where I served from 2014 to 2023.

My first car in Taiwan was a Honda Civic, which I gradually upgraded to a Ford Escort, a Volvo, and a BMW 7 Series. Automotive technology has made great strides in the past 20 or 30 years, and now, there is nearly not as much difference between small and large models. Edith learned to drive after we moved to Kansas City, which is something she had never done in Taiwan.

As you can see, I have a habit of driving nice cars because I feel good when I drive them, and safety is my top priority. Before moving here, we purchased the first Lexus LS400 model in the United States. I sold that car to my doctor, Chip Luerding when I changed to a Mercedes S500 in 1998 and drove it until 2008. I heard later that his daughter was in an accident with that car when someone drove into the driver's seat, but she was unharmed because of the car's safety features.

The dealer offered us $500 for the car as a trade-in in 2008. Edith was unhappy with the offer and drove it for another 16 years until we bought an S580 for me in 2024. It remained a good car, especially the engine. Thirty years ago, I could feel a big difference between luxury imports and less expensive cars. Today, however, they have the same stability as luxury cars. I am sure technology has made great strides, and we would feel good driving a regular car.

Driving nice cars makes you feel good and successful, and most importantly, they are safe and long-lasting. We keep three cars at home; one is a spare in case one is unavailable. Despite the high depreciation in the first few years, we always buy new cars, not second-hand cars. However, they are worth it because they last longer. Edith always gives the best to me, so she would suffer using her old car. Since we bought a new S580, I feel happy whenever I drive it. I told the salesman they should promote another feature—if you can afford it, driving a nice car can prolong your life because it can make you happier. If you are happy, your life will last longer. Some people would not care what kind of car they drive as long as it provides transportation. It's a personal preference.

I came to the United States on an E-2 visa, which allows traders from a set list of countries with which the United States has reciprocal agreements to enter the country and set up a business. I later applied for and received my U.S. citizenship with the help of a skilled immigration lawyer, Roger Hiatt of Stinson Morrison Hecker (formerly Miler & Blume) and Mira Mdivani of Mdivani Corporate Immigration Law. Although I have lived here since 1995, I waited until 2008 to become a citizen. I needed to play by the rules, wait my turn, and do everything legally.

I also used Roger Hiatt to bring our nanny to care for our daughter. After we changed our visa status, she would not be legally allowed to stay here, which is one reason we delayed applying for citizenship. A helper at home is extremely important for working families such as ours who spend a lot of tie working. We also consulted with our local attorney, Rusty Leffel, who was very specific about the law. Because our nanny worked and lived in our home, it was essential to have clear employment guidelines that didn't conflict with labor laws. In other words, she worked eight hours a day on weekdays and had Saturdays and Sundays off. Although I believed that different laws might allow for a nanny or domestic helper, I took my attorney's advice. For instance, because she lived in the house, we specified her working hours and time off, as well as rules such as not bothering her when her door was closed, except in an emergency. We also encouraged her to become involved in the local Filipino community so she could make friends. Several years later, a prominent Taiwanese person who lived here abused the rules, and it eventually became a big news story that we saw in the Kansas City newspaper. They even held her nanny's passport, which is illegal. We wanted to do everything legally and avoid even a hint of impropriety.

Immigration is a hot topic in the United States right now. As a proud immigrant, I welcome people who want to do things right and contribute to American society. However, many people are looking for a shortcut to the American dream. As Tom Zillner, the founder of DuraComm, told me in 1995, "Some companies can hire people coming from Mexico. They are illegal immigrants. If you catch them and send them back, they return next week or next month." DuraComm, like my other companies, made sure every employee we hired was legally authorized to work in the United States.

I was both surprised and shocked to discover that the U.S. government is so loose with our southern border, and enemy combatants could cross into our country undetected. You should meet specific criteria to become a U.S. citizen, and I hope I have set a good example. I had some success in my career and am fortunate to live comfortably, and I am also thankful that I could immigrate to the United States and contribute in some small way. As a U.S. citizen now,
I believe we should welcome immigrants who will contribute to our culture and help maintain a high standard of living for everyone.

At the same time, however, I am opposed to people coming to the United States illegally instead of following the rules as I and many others have done. I like to live in a society of educated, hardworking, high-quality citizens who help improve our nation. Too many people now come into the country illegally, fail to assimilate into our culture, and expect the U.S. government to take care of them. Even people from China and South America now are illegally coming across our southern border. I have read that they first travel to Ecuador and then walk through Colombia, Panama, and Mexico to our border, which is not only illegal but dangerous.

I see many immigrants to the United States, especially from mainland China, who become citizens but still feel that they belong to their home country. I would challenge them with this question: If the United States were at war, which side would you support? I support the United States, not Taiwan (of course, the two countries are strong allies, so this would never happen). However, many Chinese immigrants would support China.

Although more Chinese people are immigrating to Kansas City, few Taiwanese remain. I give everyone I meet a positive impression of my home nation by working hard, getting involved in community organizations, and donating my time and money however I can. It is easy to get involved by volunteering your time or by donating $50, $100, or whatever you can afford.

After renting at first while Edith had our first baby in 1993 we purchased a large house in Briarcliff West, a new development in the Northland, part of the city north of the

Missouri River and near Kansas City International Airport. I bought a house there because Jim Price, who worked for Payless Cashways, lived there and recommended it. I had learned that the parts of Kansas City north and south of the Missouri River were like different countries.

Our house was the model home and the third to be sold in the upscale subdivision. It was located at 43rd Terrace and North Mulberry Road, near the home of Kay Barnes, who was mayor of Kansas City at the time. The developers, Charles and Patty Garney, were pleased to be able to sell the house while they were away for the summer. We became close friends as I attended many events in their home, and Charles introduced me to several community organizations with which I became involved.

As I acclimated to a new city, my business interests also kept me busy. I continued to operate Transworld Products, which I had started in the late 1980s. Peterson Manufacturing in suburban Grandview, Mo., was our large customer, and it eventually purchased the company in August 1991. Once again, I was fortunate to work with good people, and the owner, Don Armacost, became a friend. After selling Transworld Products, I moved Top Innovations to Riverside, close to our home in Briarcliff West.

Because we were doing a lot of business importing ceiling fans for Payless Cashways, we decided to develop a new type of control. Here is how it worked: If you had a high ceiling and wanted to change the fan speed, you had to pull a long string, so we invented a switch to control the speed. If you turned the switch on and off two or three times, it gave a signal to the ceiling fan to change the speed or turn on the fan lights. It was a good idea, but we didn't sell many of them. We got a patent, but it didn't work out. Then, 10 or 15 years later, another ceiling fan company adopted the same technology. We were not involved in any way, but that was our first patent under our company name.

In 2001, Jim Price left Payless Cashways, which had closed its import division, to work for us. We had an import company called Mitco USA that focused on serving Payless Cashways' import business, so he basically continued doing the same work he had previously done, except now he worked for me.

Steve Porter, the director of Payless Cashways, also left and worked for other DIY companies before joining Mitco USA around 1999. He was well-connected with many U.S. vendors who wanted to sell their products to the companies for which Steve worked, such as Payless Cashways. After he joined Mitco USA, a friend who worked for a big hardware store chain approached him, and we developed an import line for them.

I took Steve and Jim to China, particularly the Shanghai area, and we also traveled together on Steve's first trip to Taiwan. After arriving at CSK Airport, we went directly to Taichung without staying in Taipei because all the hand-tool factories were there. That evening, the 1999 Chi-Chi earthquake, with a magnitude of 7.6, struck near our hotel in Taichung. The destruction was massive, with 2,415 people dying in 106 seconds. We stayed in a high-rise hotel with around 12 floors. My bed moved from right to left and left to right for 106 seconds. We went down and tried to sleep on the ground without much success. The next day, we visited one or two factories without much damage. I bet this was the first time Steve experienced an earthquake.

We found several tool manufacturers, evaluated their quality, and developed an imported tool line for this customer. After a successful presentation to their buyer, they decided to purchase from us. Unfortunately, however, at that time, Jim and Steve had opened a company behind my back and asked the customer to place orders with their new company. Because Steve had overseen purchasing for Payless Cashways, he had relationships with many key manufacturers. We traveled to China to visit factories, order all samples, and perform many other business tasks. Although he worked for me and I paid his salary, he planned to take my business away. I learned that he told a company in Chicago for which they wanted to import hand tools, "Don't place your order with Mitco USA, but place it with my new company instead." Just like that, he not only quit my company but tried to take a key client with him.

Then, they both quit my company. After I heard this story, I contacted one of the best local law firms, Polsinelli, and worked with Terry Kilroy. Terry told me that the government encourages people to start their own businesses in Missouri, so it might be hard for me to stop them. I didn't mind that they left and started a new company to compete with me; however, they needed to compete fairly. Using my resources and connections to travel to the Far East was unethical and not fair competition.

I told Terry that I wanted to take them to court as a matter of principle, and there was a risk that I might lose. They had everything to lose with their new company, while I had my other businesses. They also hired a large law firm, Husch Blackwell Sanders, and we finally agreed that they would pay me a percentage of their business for the next three years. I dropped that tool line, moved on to more meaningful products, and later heard that their business didn't last long, but they eventually went their own ways.

I always tell people we need to do everything ethically because God is watching us. I have always prioritized loyalty and honesty, even if it may have cost me in the short term. Although the financial compensation was agreeable, getting over the feeling of being betrayed by a trusted employee took longer. If Jim Price had been loyal to me, he probably would have become a key employee in DuraComm and other ventures. I later heard that Jim worked briefly for Peterson Manufacturing but was not there long.

My strong relationships with Kansas City businesses served me well as I transitioned from Taiwan to the U.S. Eventually, I transitioned to marketing my own products under my own company name. Thanks to Singer's decision *not* to purchase one of my products, I would enjoy a long, stressful—but ultimately rewarding—day on QVC.

When I lived in Braircliff West, Riverside, I was Grand Marshall of the parade.
Our family was in the car.

The Mayor of Riverside, Missouri, Becky Burch, visited me at the Top Innovations office.

CHAPTER 4: PICKING UP STEAM

It has often been said that the Chinese word for "crisis" combines two characters, "danger" and "opportunity." Although this is not entirely correct, it is a good description of how a difficult start in the steamer business ended successfully.

When I was working with Singer, the company asked me to develop a floor clothes steamer. At that time, the U.S. company Jiffy dominated the market with a steamer that sold for more than $250. I worked with an engineer to design an alternative steamer that worked just as well for a lot less money, with a manufacturing cost of just $28. I invested substantial time and money to design it and finish the mold. Jiffy is made with a high-quality die-cast case, but our design used PC plastic material, which substantially reduced the cost. Although a plastic mold costs much more than a metal case, the material cost is much lower.

It all looked like a profitable opportunity on paper—until Singer told me, "Oh, we decided not to buy it." Perhaps because of their iconic brand name, they decided they wanted to purchase a steamer manufactured in a Scandinavian country such as Denmark or Sweden, not in China. By then, I had invested too much time and money to back out. So, I decided to turn a potential crisis into an opportunity. If Singer didn't want to buy my steamer, I would have to sell it myself. I began selling steamers to U.S. companies under my brand name, Steamfast and enjoyed great success. As it turned out, Singer unknowingly may have done me a favor. But first, I had to deal with another potential setback.

After successfully importing the steamers from China and selling them, I received a letter from a Chinese company saying, "Mr. Lee, we have a steamer patent, and you are infringing on it. You should stop production." I thought that was crazy. I consulted with two Kansas City attorneys, Bryan Stanley and Ed Marquette of Kutak Rock LLP. Ed was a Harvard Law School graduate, and even more impressively, he was blind. Nevertheless, he could do anything that anyone else does and perhaps even do it better, including dancing with his wife at one of my parties. I was similarly impressed when I met another blind man, David Westbrook, when he invited me to lunch at Plaza III on the Country Club Plaza; I enjoyed my lunch and was inspired by him. Later, I saw him several times at the Man of the Month Fraternity, where we were both members.

Ed Marquette and Bryan Stanley, his partner who assisted me, said we should research the material the other company used in its manufacturing. It confirmed what I already knew, that I had already manufactured and marketed the product before they had applied for a patent. This event occurred after we had been shipping the steamers for one or two years, and they were becoming more popular. Because our design was new, they copied our product and leaflet and applied for a design patent. Design patents deal with product design, while utility patents deal with the function of design and are much harder to get approved. I told my attorney that we should fight back and demand that they withdraw their patent. In addition, we first advertised this model before they even applied for a patent.

We responded that we had already produced and sold our product before they applied for a patent. In fact, they copied our product. Fortunately, we found that our advertisement showed the date, so they agreed that we could ship. I asked my attorney to sue them back and ask them to withdraw the patent. My attorney told me that because we did not sell to the Chinese market, we didn't care as long as they allowed us to export it. You never know the legal issues in China. Sometimes, even if you are right, you may be in trouble.

I believe they used their patent to sell to the local Chinese market, for which I didn't have a patent at that time. We had no problem producing and shipping products from China to the United States. Although I asked my attorney to ask them to withdraw their patent, he suggested not fighting back. As a result, we allowed them to continue owning the Chinese patent if we could continue shipping to the U.S. market.

Another time, one of my large U.S. customers placed an order for five shipping containers of steamers. Unfortunately, Jecar, the factory I used in China, always seemed to be in financial trouble and asked me to pay for merchandise in advance because of their financial situation. However, my advisors warned me that I always wanted to help them and support the factory. As it turned out, the factory shortcut the process. These loans eventually added up to several hundred thousand U.S. dollars.

I later learned that the factory owner owed a great deal of money to several vendors, and a local judge's son was also a creditor. The judge responded by seizing the five containers and placing seals on them.

The owner called and said, "Benny, I really need another $200,000."

"I already paid for the shipment and can't pay again," I replied.

"Well," he said, "if you pay me, I can release the containers."

"You already owe me a lot of money, and I can't pay you again," I told him. "I already have exceeded the limit of what I can do."

The story gets even stranger from there. It turns out his secretary was a spy for the judge and was placed in her position to keep an eye on the company's finances. Because our business was growing and we placed large orders, the secretary thought Jecar wanted to produce and ship a great deal of products and then declare bankruptcy, which wasn't true. So, the judge sealed the five containers. After I told the owner I could not send him more money, he lied to his secretary, saying he needed to ask his uncle for money. But he returned to Taiwan to escape; otherwise, he might have been sentenced to jail. The secretary informed the judge, which is why he sealed the containers.

At that time, if someone owed you money, you could simply show up and take whatever you could—even the office chairs. Fortunately, my containers were sealed so no one could take them. The court held a public auction for the bankrupt company. Whoever submitted the highest bid would be awarded all of the merchandise, probably obtaining it for a much lower cost than the true market value.

Edith contacted a friend in Taiwan who had a high-level connection in China, Zen Qinghong, who was then the vice president of China. He referred my Taiwanese friend to the judge who was overseeing the case. He had to meet with the judge in a sauna to have a man-to-man talk.

He used his connections to set up a discussion with a high-level official in the Shanghai security department. He then arranged for him to meet with a judge in Shenzhen, who told him how to handle the matter.

"OK, let's do this," the judge said. "When the bid is published, you need to bring 20,000 in Chinese currency, or RMB 20,000." Everyone showed up with RMB 20,000. But 20 minutes before the auction started, they increased the amount to RMB 50,000. We knew this in advance and had brought the proper amount of cash. Although two teams appeared to be bidding, both worked for me, so we got our merchandise back. However, there was still the matter of safely shipping it to the United States.

The judge told us that the local people near the factory had a lot of power and that they might rob our truck if we took the goods away from the factory. "Don't worry," he said. They arranged for a military soldier with a gun to go with the truck. After a long, expensive ordeal, we finally got our merchandise back, transferred production to another factory, and later shipped it to the United States to satisfy our customers. But even to ship out those containers, we also needed to pay special people to do it legally. In other words, we paid customs to allow us to ship. This was how the Chinese way worked.

The factory always borrowed money from me. Everyone in the industry knows this story, which is both bad and good. The good part is that appliance factories in China, especially the ones that made steamers or related products, knew I had a lot of money and supported them financially. Although Jecar still owed me hundreds of thousands of dollars when they went bankrupt, I also made a lot from working with them.

My later adventure with the steamers, selling them on QVC, was also stressful but much more enjoyable. When I came to the United States, I felt I needed to create a product for my company, Top Innovations. I started developing a new clothes steamer with our own design for the U.S. market. It was still an entirely new product for consumers.

I teamed up with Les Boll and Randy Tosh to offer my steamer on QVC. I knew Les from Commerce Bank, from which he had retired after overseeing international accounts. He had a great deal of international experience from traveling to Europe a long time ago and told fascinating stories, such as comparing the styles of toilets in Russia with those in Western nations. Les was a significant business figure, and I enjoyed his company whenever I visited Kansas City. Randy later left our partnership team to become senior director of U.S. market development for the Australia Trade Commission. He was responsible for developing the U.S. market for Australian exports and attracting U.S. capital investment in Australia. Unfortunately, he passed away a long time ago.

Steamfast was the first steamer sold on QVC, and they first featured it around 1999. After starting with a small order, they continued to purchase more products after seeing how the audience responded. Randy previously had worked with QVC, so he knew how it operated and how to get our products on the network. In 2002, they told us, "Hey, we need to do a promotion—Today's Special Value." They asked me to design a new model, which is not uncommon. If not, viewers would complain about it being less expensive than what they had paid. We needed to make a new model with a new tool, which costs around $50,000.

Good things happen when I give to a worthy cause without expecting anything in return. The International Houseware Association's annual show in Chicago is one of the industry's largest and most prestigious events. Participation is mandatory, not optional if you want to be a player in this market. I have always found it a valuable experience, as much for informal networking as for the official agenda.

In 2005, because one of the association's secretaries had breast cancer, a fundraising dinner was held on the first night of the show to support cancer research. Many people in the industry knew and loved her, so the dinner was well attended, and many guests were prepared to write large checks.

One auction item was a dinner for 10 people at the home of the QVC president in Pennsylvania. That appealed to me because about 40 percent of my business was with QVC. Not only that but the meal would be prepared by the famous

Chinese chef Ming Tsai, who studied cuisine in France. He is as smart as he is talented. Ming Tsai studied mechanical engineering at Yale University before opening a highly successful restaurant on the East Coast. He had such a sterling reputation that former President Barack Obama later asked him to be the chef for a state dinner with President Xi Jingping of China. I had sponsored a table for the dinner and eagerly joined in the bidding at $8,000. It quickly soared to $10,000, $12,000, $15,000—but we were just getting warmed up. "Benny, it's just a dinner," a friend said. "Why are you bidding so much?" "I am helping out a good cause," I replied. I also had something else in mind. I already had decided that I wanted to submit the high bid, regardless of how much it cost.

One by one, the other bidders dropped out until only two of us were left: an executive with Homedics, which is a large company, and me, who owned a much smaller business. Neither of us was ready to give up, so we kept raising the price until the bid stood at $28,000. At that point, the auctioneer intervened. "We can't keep doing this all night," she said. "You both get a dinner for $28,000, so it's $56,000." She was very smart to propose this solution.

Although I was not nearly as well known in the industry as my friendly competitor, many people learned my name that evening. When I later left the restroom, several people approached me and asked, "Is that you?"

After I returned to Kansas City, a QVC secretary called to schedule a date for our dinner. I had an idea. "Do you think any QVC merchandising people or buyers would like to go to the dinner?" I asked. "Of course," she replied. "They never see the president at home." I had her invite people for me, which was an unusual thing to do.

When the big day came, Edith, three sales team members, and I flew to Philadelphia. We spent the afternoon visiting QVC and discussing our Steamfast steamer. Although our meetings usually consisted of only the buyer and our team, this time, top members of the purchasing department also attended, including the merchandise manager. The purchase decision is usually the buyer's job. This time, the merchandise manager encouraged him to buy more products and gave me more opportunities. The merchandise manager turned to the buyer and said, "Why don't you consider this item for our regular orders?"

I didn't think about our conversation during that evening's dinner, which five QVC employees also attended. Ming Tsai was an excellent chef who knew how to present the food and pair it with the perfect wine. It was first class all the way, as you might expect for a meal costing $2,800 per person. I slept well that night, knowing I had contributed to a worthy cause. And I felt even better about my contribution the next morning when QVC placed an order for $1.2 million worth of steamers with a profit margin of about $500,000. This order was a great return on the investment of a $28,000 donation to a worthwhile cause.

I also use this example to tell friends that God will take care of you when you do good things. Through my donation, I could not only make a big sale but also help fight breast cancer and even enjoy a wonderful meal at the home of the QVC president.

The Steamfast steamer had many advantages, such as being a new product in the market and being environmentally friendly, which is why QVC selected it. We enjoyed several successful years selling different types of steamers on QVC, including one for cleaning. It was a completely different type of product because it needed high pressure to push out the steam for cleaning, which required several extra safety features.

The Steamfast steamer, Ginsu 2000 knives, Handy Stitch sewing machine, and Tiny Tailor sewing machine turned out to be the most successful products of my career. From Singer canceling its order to the patent challenge to the success with QVC, it provided a crash course in running a business to rival any college program.

One of the most valuable lessons I have learned is that the three most important things in business are having a good accountant, a good banker, and a good lawyer. Four attorneys in particular—Marshall Miller, Larry Blume, Roger Hiatt, and Rusty Leffel—were especially helpful in both my business and immigration to the United States. Later, attorney Bob Levy helped me with the complicated transaction of selling my business and legal compliance when I ran DuraComm. Again, despite the high fees, it is important to have a good lawyer.

The IRS never audited me during my many years in business. They may have had questions from time to time, but my accountant always took care of it. I always congratulated my accountant for doing a good job. My accountant is conservative—perhaps even too conservative at times for my taste—but I never minded because I wanted my financials to be sound. Although this concept may be wrong, I believe it was sometimes better to pay more tax than was required than to take shortcuts.

One time, the city of Kansas City sent a letter asking me to pay a few thousand dollars in additional tax. My accountant, Wayne Bridges, advised me to go ahead and pay because it is hard to fight a bureaucracy. However, because I knew several influential people there through my community involvement, I was able to resolve the issue with just one phone call. Wayne was impressed when I showed him the document showing I no longer owed money. Nevertheless, I would much rather have my accountant protect me than run into a problem I would have to face.

I also have a good banker who is very realistic. I had about a $2 million line of credit, but I understood that the bank always has your guarantee, and if you do not pay back your loan, they will take everything. I had brought some money to the United States when I came here, but Top Innovations had a loan from the bank for more than $1 million, and Edith was worried. "Benny, you owe the bank a million dollars," she said. "But our business is growing, and we have inventory," I replied. However, I really appreciate the fact that she is financially conservative.

I also learned that banking can sometimes be a cold business, even when I have a strong personal relationship with the banker. I once borrowed $1 million from Commerce Bank, using my office building as collateral. I assumed everything was fine until the day two guys came to me and said, "Hey, Benny, we don't want to loan any more money to you."

I am an open, honest person. However, as my attorney Bob Levy said, it's not always necessary to tell the entire story when dealing with a bank. During a conversation with my bankers, whom I considered to be friends, I told them about my bad investment in Spain, in which I lost $2 million in two years. This is why they no longer wanted to loan money to me. Bob Levy, my attorney, was surprised to hear this. He recommended calling bank President Jonathan Kemper, whom I knew from our Man of the Month fraternity. Instead, I contacted Great Western Bank, which was happy to loan me the money. The two men from Commerce later said they felt bad about the situation, but I told them it turned out fine for me and my businesses.

Despite that situation, however, I generally have a good relationship with banks. Even if you have money and inventory, you still need a bank because most businesses here do not pay cash. The terms are 30 days or sometimes 60 or even 90 days. QVC had ordered 16,000 pieces for their special value and didn't pay upfront. By contrast, I didn't get credit from the manufacturers in China, but I had to pay in full before they made the shipment. Sometimes, they ship first but give you only 15 days to pay. So, you need a bank.

I also do not cut corners when hiring a lawyer, which paid off when my steamer business was doing well. I was selling a new product to Hancock Fabric, a large retailer. Bill Emerson, president of Singer and later worked for me as president of

Top Innovations, introduced me to this client. Bill had resigned from Singer to protect himself in the wake of several scandals following its purchase by SemiTech (the owner eventually went to prison in Canada). Bill had worked for several Chinese manufacturers before joining my company. He is a smart man, and we remain close friends today. I also became good friends with Barry Inglis, the general manager of Singer Canada.

The product was being manufactured by Jecar, a factory in China owned by a Taiwanese company that owed me quite a bit of money. Hancock Fabric placed an order for five containers, so we rushed the product into production. We applied for UL certification, and everything was approved except the FPI or factory production inspection. Although the product was approved, the UL inspector needed to be there for the first production. If it passed, the factory would be allowed to put a UL label on the product.

However, this factory mistakenly (or intentionally) placed the UL label on the product without the FPI, which UL discovered in the port in Los Angeles. They wanted to confiscate the shipment, which was five containers and represented a lot of money. Still, they later agreed to let us ship the containers back to China and relabel them. Because Hancock Fabric had customers waiting for the product, I had the factory manufacture another five containers so I could fulfill the order.

Businesses in the United States have step-by-step processes, and you need to do everything legally. By contrast, in China at that time, they sometimes gave you money under the table. But now it is different. In China, everything is "Yes, sir, yes, sir. No problem." This often can be translated as, "There may not be a problem for us, but there may be a problem for you." And "Yes" means "I heard what you said," not necessarily, "I agree with you."

Thanks to the support of my accountant, banker, and lawyer, as well as suppliers, customers, and business associates, I found success running a business that spanned American and Asian cultures. It was not always easy, but I would not trade anything for the experiences I had and the people I met along the way. It meant a lot to me that the Kansas City business community embraced me as one of their own.

In 2014, I was honored to be named Philanthropist of the Year in Kansas City, which was not an easy accomplishment in such a charitable community. I had donated $1 million to the new birthing center at AdventHealth Shawnee Mission, where our daughter had been born, and the president of their foundation nominated me. It was even more impressive when I looked back at the names of previous winners, who were a Who's Who of Kansas City business and civic leaders. The award itself was heavy, so I joked about it to make my point as I spoke to about 1,000 people during the presentation at the Marriott Hotel.

"I am thankful to be named philanthropist of the year, but this is too heavy for me," I said. "The weight of the trophy is heavy, but the name also is heavy. When you say philanthropist, you are talking about someone such as Bill Gates or Warren Buffett. You should say, 'This is a good man.'

So, I like to call it the Goodman Award instead of philanthropist, so you can call me Benny Goodman."

Everyone laughed at my joke, including Landon Rowland, the owner of Lead Bank and a community leader, who said he almost fell off his chair in laughter. Leo Morton, who was UMKC chancellor at the time, told me, "Benny, you are a comedian."

I had arrived in my new home with big dreams, and now I felt fully accepted as part of the community. Although I still had other businesses to start and products to sell, I was more determined than ever to give more of my time, talent, and treasure to the place I called home.

CHAPTER 5: GIVING BACK

When I moved to Kansas City, I was fortunate to become involved with several people who were good role models for not only running a successful business but also giving back to the community.

Real estate developer Charles Garney has been one of them. He not only sold me my home in Briarcliff West but also became a close friend who helped me connect with the philanthropic community in Kansas City. It is an honor to be asked to give back and help out however I can. People often ask me, "Benny, why do you give money to so many organizations?" The short answer is that it feels good to give. When you do good things, you feel good.

A story I told when I received the Philanthropist of the Year award illustrates my point: "When I do good, I feel good, my business grows, and even my hair grows." (I had started getting hair implants then, so my hair really did grow.) A good speech entertains people and makes them laugh while making an important point, and everyone enjoyed my joke.

I have heard it said that some people use drugs because of a chemical reaction in their brain that makes them feel better. I have found that you can get the same good feeling, without the dangers of using drugs, simply by helping others. People sometimes assume that I give because it will benefit my business. However, although much of my giving is in the

Kansas City area, most of my customers have been on the East Coast, West Coast, or overseas.

Although I always believed that my business would prosper if I were generous, it was never just a bottom-line transaction. It is important to me to not just write a check and forget about it but to also get involved with the organizations I support to gain a better understanding and make new friends. When you have friends, you become comfortable and feel that this is your home. The motivation behind giving is as important as the dollar figure on the check. For example, when I have dinner with friends, I always offer to pay. It may be a small amount, but sometimes they will remember me better if I pay for dinner. However, I never intend to use money to buy their friendship.

My lifelong dream was to live in the United States. Moving here turned out well for me, my family, and my businesses, and Kansas City has embraced me with open arms. I consider it a privilege to give back to my adopted home, and I realize I could never give more than my family and I have received. I have already decided to stay here for the rest of my life, so making connections and investing in my community is a good practice. Home is where you have friends and family.

Looking back, it is interesting how many similarities there are between being an effective philanthropist and a successful businessperson. One thing I quickly learned after moving to the United States is how many opportunities there are to give, which is something I observe every time I open my mail. No one has the resources to support every worthy cause. Just as in business, it is necessary to have a strategic plan built around core values such as, in my case, music and education.

It also is important to have trusted mentors. Although I had done some charitable work in Taiwan, I had a smaller social circle. I didn't become serious about philanthropy until I moved to Kansas City. Many of my donations in Taiwan were made through my mother, who donated under my name. Although I would not have considered myself wealthy at that time, my family had enough money to live comfortably, with enough left over to begin giving.

One of the first people I reached out to after moving to Kansas City was Elizabeth Chu, head of the local Taiwanese consulate, which works with six Midwestern states. It was interesting to learn how the consulate came to be in Kansas City (although it has since relocated to Denver). Chiang Kai-shek's son had been in trouble for his behavior in Taiwan, so he sent him to study here at Park University, where he later opened a consulate in the city.

When I came to Kansas City in 1999, there had been a flood, and the consulate sought contributions to assist the victims. As I recall, I donated about $1,500 or $2,500. Along with helping those in need, I received some excellent advice in return.

"Benny," she said, "with all this mail asking for money, you need to choose what you want to support because you certainly can't support everything."

This donation strengthened my relationship with the consul, who eventually asked me to become involved with the Consulate Corps of Kansas City. Through this involvement, I made many lifelong friends, such as Sharon Valasek of the Czech Republic, Ross Marine of Slovakia, and Robert Serra of Italy. Once again, this showed that generous people receive far more than they give.

After that first step, Charles Garney showed me how to become a committed philanthropist who supported the community and did so strategically so it would have the greatest impact. After I had purchased a house from him, he held a fundraising event in his home for the Kansas City Chorale. Because he knew I loved music, he invited me. One auction item was an opportunity to be a guest conductor, and I submitted a high bid. I had a fun time conducting the chorale. Still, more importantly, I helped support one of the city's leading arts organizations.

Charles later introduced me to the United Way of Greater Kansas City. I appreciated its structure because donors could help many worthy charities by making a single contribution. I also wanted my family to support the group and understand that there are many people in need in the community and that not everyone enjoys our family's privileges.

One day, when my children were young, I asked the United Way people to take our family to visit the underprivileged. This was a learning experience for all of us. "This shows how lucky you are," I told them. "Many children have no parents, and poor families must depend on help from a United Way agency."

I became more deeply involved in the United Way. Pete Levi, president of the Greater Kansas City Chamber of Commerce, asked me to become a board member in 2003.

They wanted to make the board more diverse, which provided an opportunity to get to know such important civic leaders as Donald Hall Jr. of Hallmark Cards. I met as many people and learned as much as possible. I especially enjoyed being part of the Leadership Exchange, a group of 100 leaders who spent two or three days in different cities. As a bonus, I got to know those leaders from Kansas City better as we traveled together.

Although my motivation was to help others, serving on the board helped me build relationships with some of the most powerful members of the Kansas City business community, such as top executives of Sprint (now T-Mobile) and Blue Cross Blue Shield. My friend Bob Levy remembers those days of serving together and the long-term relationship that developed from it.

"Benny and I were on the board of directors of the United Way of Greater Kansas City for several years, and I admired his commitment to the organization, his entrepreneurial approach to the issues we faced, and his ties to the Asian community. When I became board chairman, I invited him to lunch to get to know him better. At our luncheon, he told me that after lunch, he was going to see a member of a prominent Kansas City law firm because he had received an offer to purchase one of his businesses and was going to need an experienced transaction attorney to assist him. I said, Benny, don't do that. I'm an experienced transaction attorney, and I can help you. As we discussed the matter, he became comfortable with my approach. He indicated that my work with the United Way had given him confidence in me. He canceled his meeting

with the other firm, and we successfully navigated the sale of his business. I continued to represent him for several decades until his last operating business was sold."

I became even more heavily involved by joining the United Way Tocqueville Society. This exclusive group is named after the famous French author Alexis de Tocqueville, who is best known for writing the influential book Democracy in America in the mid-1800s. As an immigrant myself, I could relate to his descriptions of the United States, its citizens, and what makes it such a special place. At the time I joined, members were required to donate at least $5,000, although larger donations would give you a higher position. The Tocqueville Society has around 130 members in the Kansas City area. We met quarterly at interesting places throughout Kansas City, such as MRI Global, which conducts classified research for the government and military. As always, I felt that by being asked to join. I received far more than I gave.

One lesson I learned about philanthropy is that the more you give, the more you will be asked to contribute. A corresponding lesson is that it becomes harder to say no after you gain a reputation for generosity. That happened in 2007 when United Way President Tom Duggard casually asked, "Do you know Min Kao?" "Of course," I replied. "Can you introduce us?" he asked.

Such seemingly innocent questions can lead to large commitments. Min was born in Zhushan, Nantou, a small town in Taiwan, and studied electrical engineering at the National Taiwan University. Like me, he immigrated to the

Kansas City area, where he became the co-founder of Garmin. It has grown to a $41.75 billion business that manufactures GPS technology for automotive, aviation, marine, and outdoor applications. As a result, Min's worth is now estimated at $6.9 billion.

At the time, it was not as big as today, but it grew quickly. Despite being one of the most successful businesspeople in the city, Min tended to keep a low profile. The United Way president wanted to introduce Min to the organization and see if he would like to become involved. He asked what Min was interested in. "Min Kao is from Taiwan and loves his home country," I told him. "We can use that to grow the Tocqueville Society," he replied.

The plan was for Min to underwrite a one-week, all-expenses-paid tour of Taiwan for 10 couples, including business-class airline tickets. Five couples' names would be drawn from a list of new members as an incentive to join, and five existing members would join them, for a total of 10 couples. The cost for Min would be around $100,000.

I agreed to arrange a meeting at Garmin headquarters in Olathe, a Kansas City suburb. The meeting went well, although Min didn't officially commit to the plan. I later received a phone call from the United Way president. "Benny, we are having a United Way event tomorrow, and I would like to announce the Taiwan promotion."

When I followed up with Min, I found he had a new twist in mind. "OK, Benny, this is the condition," he said. "First, you need to go and lead the group, not me. Second, you need to share with me."

My first reaction was, "I am happy that Min Kao wants to share with me because he is very wealthy." I was joking, of course, because my wealth in no way compares with his. He is a billionaire, and I am just a regular person. But no, he wanted to share expenses, which came to $50,000 each. I didn't particularly like that idea, but I accepted it, so we each paid $50,000 and enjoyed a successful trip.

The United Way Taiwan held a welcome reception for our group when we arrived. I also asked two good business friends at Mean Well and Poly Way to donate to United Way and attend the reception. I had my office work with a travel agency in Taiwan to arrange for a guide to accompany our group. We visited the most famous sites in the nation, including the night market and Longshan Temple, where my family had a long and deep connection. The group also experienced Taiwanese culture by visiting the National Palace Museum, which has priceless art objects, some 3,000 or 4,000 years old. Despite a small earthquake, the group enjoyed visiting the beautiful east coast of Taiwan. Min graciously gave them a tour of the Garmin factory in the Taipei area, and afterward, he and his wife were hosts for a nice dinner.

I considered the trip a success because many of the guests would not have had an opportunity to visit Taiwan otherwise. Spending an entire week together, from breakfast through dinner, gave us an opportunity to get to know each other and build lasting relationships. Edith and I held a Tocqueville Society party in our home after we returned, and the Kansas City Star ran a story saying Taiwan had become a tool for a United Way fundraiser. United Way later gave me an award for my role in making the trip possible. Beth Burke from the organization expressed her gratitude in a letter:

"*Benny worked tirelessly with me for months on details of the trip, including working with United Way of Taiwan to cohost an event while we were there so we could learn about their work. It was a memorable experience in many ways, including the excitement of surviving a typhoon. As the United Way of America worked to increase its international efforts, I was asked to share this wonderful example with my cohorts at a national conference the following year, encouraging them to do the same. The opportunity built strong relationships among our donors and a special bond for these couples with United Way.*"

Another time, I had the honor of entertaining Kansas City Mayor Pro Tem Bill Skaggs and Jody Edgerton of the Sister Cities Association while they were visiting Taiwan Tainan, the ancient capital of Taiwan, and Kansas City are sister cities. Tainan features a warm climate, with many business opportunities readily available. It is located on the southwest coast of Taiwan and served as the island's capital from 1683 to 1887 under the Qing dynasty. I enjoyed showing them around Taiwan and touring factories for electric bicycles, solar panels, and other products. Among the other highlights were dinner with my good friend Milo of Poly Way, lunch with Tainan City Mayor Tain-Tsair Hsu, and a visit to the high-tech industry zone and Kaohsiung Port. One year later, a Tainan business group led by the mayor reciprocated by visiting Kansas City and attending a reception at my office, which many city leaders attended. I love these types of international activities.

As I became better known in the business and philanthropic communities, doors continued to open for me. I focused most of my efforts on business, education, and arts organizations. One way I got to know the other members informally was through events at a member's home, such as the CEO of Cerner (now Oracle), a pioneer in electronic medical records.

In 2013, I made a substantial donation to fund the Benny and Edith Lee Atrium in the new birthing center at AdventHealth Shawnee Mission. This hospital holds a special place in our hearts because our first daughter, Elizabeth, was born there after 34 hours of labor and received exceptional care. The hospital's foundation approached me, and although it was a stretch, we felt it was something we could do. We paid part of the donation upfront, and the remainder will be paid through our estate. They heavily promoted our contribution to inspire others to give, and a news release about it ran in more than 30 Midwestern newspapers.

I had to think long and hard before making this donation. I am not a qualified donor who had an extra $1 million to contribute. However, they gave me a flexible option of paying the remaining contribution through our estate. Although the medical center was excited about the gift, I thanked them for the opportunity because other people could have stepped up and contributed instead of me. Even though $1 million is a large amount of money for Edith and me, our estate—including our home—is worth far more than that. Ken Bacon, who was president and CEO at the time, was kind enough to nominate me for Philanthropist of the Year:

"*Benny approaches philanthropy in much the same way he approaches his business – with in-depth study, careful planning, and superb execution of the plan. All of this, however, he imbues with great creativity. Benny seeks to improve our community every day. He is an ideal philanthropic role model.*"

More recently, I received this email from my friend Ron Gutierrez, who is a vocalist with the Kansas City Jazz Orchestra:

"*Good morning, Benny. We just arrived with our daughter. Shyann, at the birthing center at Shawnee Mission Medical Center. She is in one of the triage rooms adjacent to your beautiful atrium. This is just a fabulous facility. Lord willing, I will meet my first grandchild (a boy!) today or possibly tomorrow. I just wanted to let you know how reassuring it has been to see your name every time we have been here, especially today. Life moves forward excellently as my sister continues her journey and my grandson begins his. Have a blessed day!*"

It reminded me yet again that you can't go wrong by doing good. Far more important than the money is the legacy we are leaving. As I told my friend. "If such a well-known place puts your name and photo in the lobby, how much is that worth each year simply as an advertising fee, $50,000 or even $100,000 per year?" These facilities will still be there 100 years from now. Your child or grandchild would be proud of it, and most importantly, it will serve as an example for them to be useful in our society. This also inspires others to do the same for their communities.

Many years from now, no one will remember what kind of car you drove or what house you lived in, but they will know that you did a good thing for a good cause. Again, I am grateful to have had this opportunity. Michael Haverty, formerly with Kansas City Southern, said he took his niece there and was surprised to see a picture of Edith and me. He emailed, "Benny, I just took my daughter to the hospital, and I saw your picture. I want to thank you. You are doing so much for Kansas City."

In fact, six of his grandchildren have been born there now. Although it was a big commitment, knowing our contribution will live on long after we are gone is encouraging.

I sometimes feel frustrated that my desire to give is bigger than my ability to donate as much as wealthier people. However, the organizations I support have graciously found ways to leverage my donations and enable a regular person like me to leave a legacy in Kansas City.

I especially welcome opportunities to help other Asians follow my path in the United States. I contributed to the Asian American Chamber of Commerce of Kansas City, and they asked me to become involved. Although it was a small group at the time, I am proud of how it has grown and added such influential companies as Hallmark, Burns & McDonnell, and UMB Bank as honorary members. It has become a highly successful organization and is doing great things in the community, such as sponsoring a scholarship. The Asian American Chamber of Commerce has given me numerous honors, most recently its emeritus award.

"*Benny's leadership as president from 2010 to 2012 was key to establishing the chamber's foundation and ensuring its continued growth and sustainability.*" Executive Director Sook Park said.

She also remembers a time when the chamber gave me an award, and I didn't exactly follow the script.

"*When Benny was president of the Asian American Chamber KC and took the stage at our 2012 awards gala, he was expected to follow a script like others on stage when addressing over 500 guests," Park said. "His speech had been prepared, but as soon as Benny began speaking, it was clear he wasn't following the script. At first, I felt a pang of worry, but that concern quickly faded. Within moments, Benny's genuine and engaging delivery won the audience's attention. He captivated the audience, making them laugh and engaging them in the event. We could not have asked for a better speech performance on stage.*"

I also have been able to pursue my interests in law enforcement and international affairs. Judge Robert Serra, whom I knew as the honorary Italian consul from the Consular Corps, invited me to join the FBI Citizens Academy, one of my interests. Past students can recommend new members, and the consul who had gone through the program, recommended me for the class of 2008. The role of the academy is to reach out to the community to help them understand what the FBI does for us so they will not be afraid of it. Recruits must be leaders in the community and pass a background check.

Members undergo three hours of training a week for 10 weeks at the local FBI headquarters in the spring and fall. We had an opportunity to shoot handguns and a rifle, and I was surprised that I did well after not having shot a gun for a long time after military training in Taiwan 50 years ago. I followed the instructions well and learned to press the trigger lightly after aiming. Otherwise, the gun would push down, and I would miss the target. Another highlight was visiting the FBI headquarters in Washington, D.C., the crime lab, and the academy in Quantico, Virginia.

At one memorable monthly speaker session, I heard Frank Abagnale, a former conman whose remarkable story is told in the book and movie *Catch Me if You Can.* After finishing his prison sentence, he served in the FBI. He later started a business that showed people how to avoid bank scams, which he said cost billions of dollars yearly.

Each Christmas from 2008 to 2019, I held a party in my home for the academy, with anywhere from 140 to 160 people attending. Among others, the SAC (Secret Agent Chief) of the FBI for the Midwest always participated and made a few remarks. Edith and I always felt it was an honor to be hosts of these events. We stopped having parties during the pandemic in 2020 but resumed them in 2023 with the Polsinelli law firm as host. People continued to tell me how much they had enjoyed the Christmas parties in our home.

One of the many nice things about Kansas City is that, if you are willing, you can get involved in many things. I also am serving my third term as a trustee with the Command and General Staff College Foundation in Fort Leavenworth, Kansas. Gabrielle Reilly, a former trustee who originally was from Australia, recommended it to me about a decade ago. Fort Leavenworth is home to the best military school in the world, and I am happy to give back in some small way. I served until July 2023, when they gave me emeritus status. I once met and had my photo taken with General Lloyd Austin, who was named defense secretary by President Joe Biden. I also met several close friends, such as General Bryan Wampler and his wife, Jennifer. We became close friends and often met during community events or music performances.

My interest in world affairs includes involvement in the International Relations Council of Kansas City. In 2005, they presented me with an International Business Award with the Japanese consul and Senator Sam Brownback of Kansas, who received an award for his humanitarian work during the tragedy in Darfur. I received the award on stage in front of about 600 people and gave a short speech.

"I am an international traveler and just came back from Shanghai last night," I said. "I visited the jazz club in Shanghai, which is amazing. There was a jazz band, the Peace Hotel Old Man Jazz Band, that is famous in China and where every member must be at least 80 years old. I went there because I love music. They play jazz, but it is not improvised.

Their jazz is very structured, much like their military. This was Communist China. Jazz is all about free expression and improvisation. How can you expect them to have this kind of skills if they are communist?"

At the time of the Gulf War, I talked about visiting Europe. "People were criticizing America and asked why we invaded Iraq," I said. "We were fighting for American values, and I don't care if I lose a customer. People said, 'How can you fight with a customer? Customers should be number one. The customer is always right.' I believe that the customer is not always right. I don't care because if I argue with or lose a customer, I will find another one, but I cannot find another America."

The audience was quiet for a few seconds before applauding. I went on speaking about all of the good things about the United States. Sen. Brownback spoke next and said, "Mr. Lee, that was a wonderful comment you made. With a strong accent, you said it better than anybody else could." Everybody laughed, and I considered his remarks to be a good compliment.

When I first came to the United States, I never dreamed I would one day speak to such a large crowd, including a U.S. senator. Although I am naturally shy, the more speeches I give, the more comfortable I become. Americans are eager to hear new perspectives and learn what immigrants say about their country.

Although I work hard to improve my English, my pronunciation is imperfect. Nevertheless, Americans are very forgiving and understand what I am trying to say, even if it may not be the best grammar. That being said, my English has improved since I moved to the United States. Rosalene, my secretary in Taiwan, had trouble understanding me on one visit, even though she majored in English. I had picked up several American slang phrases, such as "you bet." I remain diligent about writing down English words that I don't know and continuing to improve my language skills.

I also found that Americans enjoy it when you mix in a bit of humor with your speech and that they often will remember the jokes even if they forget everything else you said. One company I did business with, Mean Well, invited its customers to an event at its office in San Francisco in 2008. Each customer was given a few minutes to speak in front of about 100 people. I was the second person to talk.

"I just acquired DuraComm," I began. "A consultant came to my office to do evaluations and said, 'Mr. Lee, you are in a dangerous position because you have only one supplier. You should have more suppliers than just one—Mean Well—in case your supplier gives you trouble.'"

"You're right," I said. "Thank you very much for your advice. How is your family?"

"Fine," he replied. "I have a nice wife and good kids. Everybody is good, and my wife is really nice."

"Well, have you ever thought about if, someday, you may lose your wife? You should find another wife so you will be prepared if you lose this one. One good wife is enough."

Everybody loved that story, so I became popular in the group. They also remembered the point I wanted to make—if you have a good supplier, one is enough.

Even today, people continue to ask, "Benny, why do you give? Do you expect anything in return? Does it help your business?"

"No," I typically respond. "Most of my customers are not in Kansas City. Most of my business is with wholesalers. But when you give, you feel good, and your employees are proud to work for a generous company."

It is like a competition in which you fall behind if other people give more. I sometimes feel bad and ask why other people are not getting involved with fundraisers. They have a lot of money, but I can't judge them. They have other involvements. Kansas City is one of the most charitable cities in the United States. People give not only money but time.

Over the years of getting involved, I have established an image in our community. I try to let people know I am a good man. I am sure my kids are proud of my involvement and hope it will be an example to them. Despite giving away what, for me, was a large amount of money—or perhaps because of it—my business continued to grow and prosper.

Taiwanese Pianist Tzu-Yi Chen played Pictures at an Exhibition by Mussorgsky. Michael and Marlys Haverty were my guests.

Playing my clarinet at the Museum at Prairefire in 2017.

Sister City event at my home

CHAPTER 6: CONTINUED GROWTH

Christianity teaches that it is better to give than to receive, and I wholeheartedly agree. I know that when I help others, I am the one who benefits most. However, I have also learned that consistent giving requires a reliable revenue stream. This principle became especially clear when my accountant told me I had donated several million dollars to nonprofit organizations. All I know is that God takes care of my finances when I am generous.

Fortunately, my business ventures continued to prosper and grow with my giving. The fact that I looked for opportunities to serve my community is a big reason my businesses flourished. However, it is not directly related, and I don't have local customers because of my giving. Simply put, you can't go wrong by doing good.

Although I was trained as an electrical engineer, my most successful products were as diverse as Ginsu 2000 knives and clothes steamers. One thing they have in common is meeting a need in the marketplace. We once supplied items such as Montblanc-type pens to Time magazine for them to give to subscribers. I was amazed at the quantity they purchased.

You must always consider why customers need your product or service. For example, I don't want to sell chairs unless they are unique or different because they are readily available from various companies. Instead, from the very beginning, I ask, "What is our specialty? What makes us different?" Always find and promote the features that differentiate your product.

I once developed a pasta maker on a suggestion from an industry connection in Taiwan. I saw other companies making pasta makers and successfully selling them through infomercials. I hired an engineer to design the product, developed a mold in China, and found a factory to produce it. Rival, the Kansas City company famous for introducing the crockpot, thought it would be a good addition to its product line and contacted me through our representative, Ed Davis. We made a unique product for them under the Rival name. Rival, which supplies big retailers like Walmart, has a highly respected brand name and can sell many products. As a bonus, I held a pasta party for everyone in my neighborhood when I lived in Northland. It also was a good way to see if people liked the product.

These types of niche products could often be lucrative overseas markets. I once shipped around a million sandwich makers to Paraguay through Singer's agent. I gave them 60 days' credit, which I usually don't do, paid the manufacturer, shipped the product, and then collected payment. The products were intended for the Brazilian market. Still, because Brazil had a 35 percent import fee, they were shipped to Paraguay instead, and people were hired to carry them across the border and bypass the duty.

Once again, I learned how important it is to understand local customs and occasionally offer customers some flexibility on credit terms. However, this must be done only on a case-by-case basis. The Indian market can be challenging. Many years ago, a customer refused to pay despite having a letter of credit opened by an Indian bank. They tried to create a dispute in which they could keep the products and delay payment. Although I finally got paid six months later, it made me cautious about doing business in India again. But overall, given the many nations, customers, and products I have worked with, I consider myself fortunate.

After our successful experience with QVC, at which we sold 16,000 products as Today's Special Value in 2002, our steamer business grew exponentially. However, new risks and potential liabilities came with an expanded product line. Although clothes steamers do not require pressure, just steam, steam cleaners require a boiler to produce pressure. If it gets hot enough, it could cause an explosion, which not only could cause serious injuries but potentially put our company out of business. Because we always put safety first, we include built-in safety devices, such as a thermostat and fuse to cut off power when the temperature gets too high and a valve to release pressure. If every safety device failed simultaneously, our company would close, so we always went the extra mile to make our products safe.

In all our years in business, we had only one or two claims, which we quickly resolved. We once had a fake claim in which someone was injured by a clothes steamer and showed us the burns. However, he disappeared when we turned the claim over to our insurance company. We even had a complaint that someone had used the clothes steamer to iron while still wearing the clothes. Another person told us he could not plug in the steamer, not realizing he first had to remove the protective cover on the plug. We saw all kinds of people and had to laugh about it. Thousands of customers have enjoyed safe, efficient performance at a competitive price. Although running a business involves many risks, they are part of the price you pay for, as well as being able to enjoy the rewards.

Because Top Innovations expanded quickly, we began outgrowing our longtime headquarters in Riverside. I was fond of the area and appreciated the strong support of civic leaders. Mayor Becky Burch said I was her favorite person and honored to be named grand marshal of a local parade. Although I didn't even know what a grand marshal was then, I was grateful that they chose me. In 2005, Mayor Burch presented Edith and me with the Pinnacle Award in recognition of our contributions to the community. I always remember how many people showed up for the presentation at a 7 a.m. breakfast. Mayor Burch was a down-to-earth person who was not a traditional politician but simply someone who wanted to make Riverside a better place to live and work.

Nevertheless, when it came time to move our headquarters in 2005, we would have to explore options beyond Riverside. It would be hard to find an available space that meets the needs of our type of business. We always kept a large inventory on site. Some customers can wait for their orders, and we can ship directly, but others need their products right away, and if they had to wait too long, we would lose the order. We were looking for an existing facility with both a big office and a large warehouse, but most buildings with large warehouses had small offices in the exact location. We like having the operations office and warehouse in the same building, making resolving problems more manageable. Edith and I want to be able to physically touch the products, especially if there are technical problems.

Our search led us to a former Pfizer pharmaceutical warehouse at 6655 Troost in South Kansas City. The name "Troost" raised red flags among my friends and business associates. During racial segregation, this major north-south street had been considered a dividing line between black and white residents. More recently, people thought of it as a high-crime area. My friends told me, "Benny, Troost is no good. You might be killed. It's a dangerous place."

Nevertheless, I visited with the Southtown Council, which promoted development in the area. They said, "Oh, no, this is a very nice place." I felt comfortable moving to that area, purchased the building for $1.1 million, and spent another $1 million to remove asbestos insulation and renovate it. It had everything we needed: 10,000 square feet of office space and a 38,000-square-foot warehouse on five acres. Because we were next door to an old cemetery, I joked that it was a quiet neighborhood. This suggestion was unlike in China, where seeing graves is considered to be unlucky. Another saying in China is that Guan Chi, the phrase for the coffin, also can mean high officer or money, which implies that my position would be higher, and money would come.

Finally, when the work was completed and we moved in, we knew we had the ideal location to grow the business. We had a fresh, big space for everyone to work, a spacious cafeteria, a large conference room, and a shower. It was a place where our employees would be proud to work, and customers would enjoy visiting. As a result, we enjoyed rapid growth as we hired more than 20 employees to keep up with demand. I worked with engineers in Taiwan to develop new products, and we began exporting to Spain and other European nations, with modifications to meet international standards. We also found good customers, such as Rival, in our backyard.

When we first moved in, I visited several families in the area, gave them $50 gift cards to Gates Bar-B-Q, and told them we would be good neighbors. Despite my friends' concerns, the Troost location worked out well for us, and it was a short two-mile drive from my home. We had security cameras and a fence, but there was never a break-in during the 17 years we spent there. The only theft was an inside job, in which a young employee stole a steamer and tossed it over the fence to a friend. I let him leave my employment; I didn't turn him in to the police, although it was caught on camera. I would not have known about this theft if a neighbor to whom I had given a gift card hadn't called to tell me.

I was pleased to be able to hire two bright Park University students from Brazil, Heber Cardoso and Leandro Silva, to work at Top Innovations. Although they later returned to Brazil, we have remained close friends. Heber invited me to his wedding, and Edith and I attended his wedding party. Brazilian weddings are unique, and I loved their music, especially the bossa nova, which they played and danced to all night. As a bonus, Leandro arranged for a helicopter to fly us to visit several companies, which was a great way to avoid the Sao Paulo traffic. In the night, they took me to a music club where they played my favorite Latin bossa nova music. It gave us a lot of satisfaction to know they enjoyed their time at Top Innovations and highly respected us.

Heber also helped my daughter, Elizabeth, gain a better opinion of China. Because of Payless Cashways, I once had an opportunity to visit a wheelbarrow factory in China. I was surprised that my mobile phone worked well then. However, I was not as impressed with the toilet paper and other public facilities. I brought some back from the trip, and it was not good quality because China was poorer and less developed then, which gave Elizabeth the wrong impression.

Fortunately, that impression changed during the summer when she attended Connecticut College. Heber worked in a new company called F.C. Stone that traded commodities, first for F.C. Stone in Sao Paulo and then for the new F.C. Stone in Kansas City. He helped Elizabeth get a summer job, first in Kansas City and then in Shanghai, where they had just opened an office in the prestigious Jin Mao Tower, Economic Trading Tower. At 420 meters, it was the tallest building in China and third in the world. She lived in our apartment in Shanghai, which I had renovated a month earlier, and her impression of the country completely changed.

Although I have never considered myself a salesperson, I got more involved with the sales side of the business after we moved, such as when I attended the International Houseware Association's annual show in Chicago. I am friendly and enjoy meeting people, which are essential traits in sales. Customers always know I will be honest with them and provide a quality product at a fair price.

Anyone successful in business will be presented with multiple opportunities to purchase or invest in other companies. The key is to know which ones to pursue and which to pass up. I always do my homework, and although there are a few transactions I would not do again, I make the right decisions more often than not. I freely admit that I made mistakes, primarily because of making decisions too quickly.

The fact is, everyone is going to make mistakes. The key is how we respond, learn from them, and correct our course in the future. Edith and I always had a logical approach to business. If a problem arose, we always asked, "Why did this happen, whose fault was it, and how do we correct it?" We wanted to know who was at fault, not to blame them but to be able to trace the actual cause of the problem and find ways to prevent it from happening again.

I soon learned that this approach worked better in Taiwan than in the United States. American workers do not take criticism well and look for excuses for various cultural reasons. Although no one enjoys admitting their mistakes, this is the first step to correcting them and preventing them from recurring.

I always appreciate it when an employee comes to me and says, "Benny, I'm sorry; I made this mistake because I didn't sleep well, or I had a fight with my wife." Any reason is acceptable if it is honest. If you know the reason, you will avoid it the next time. However, this kind of accountability is unacceptable, especially in the United States. This is why I became more careful when I came to the United States and didn't criticize people in the same way. Instead, I give a hint; hopefully, people will make corrections. I also always give praise when people come to me and say, "Hey, I made a mistake." Edith is very strict, and I am softer. In many cases I open one eye and close one eye.

I made it a point to treat my staff as well as possible. For example, DuraComm originally paid 99 percent of insurance premiums for our employees and 75 percent for family members at more than $120,000 annually. Although we later had to change this to 90 percent and 50 percent because of reduced revenue, it was still generous for a small company like ours. Some small companies do not offer health insurance with such high benefits.

DuraComm proved to be a successful venture after selling Top Innovations and making what turned out to be a bad investment in Spain. I returned to my electrical engineering roots as one of four shareholders in DuraComm, supplying products such as AC/DC converters, charging systems, and power generators. I initially owned 51 percent of the company. Although a majority required 70 percent agreement, nothing could be done without my approval. I could not make any changes if two of them did not agree, but they couldn't make any changes without my approval if I disagreed.

Although I was 61 and could have retired after selling Top Innovations, I wanted to keep working and believed I understood DuraComm's challenges and how to solve them. Around 2008, I became more involved in DuraComm, and in 2011, I became sole owner. I understood the potential problems because although they made money, they relied on one source, Mean Well, and one major customer, Motorola. In other words, because Mean Well is a huge company (+$1.3b in sales), it could cut us out and approach Motorola directly, although I have a good connection with Jerry.

I grew the company from seven to 20 employees and doubled the revenue. Although we were looking for more growth after 2014, we did not get a replacement for our Motorola key item, which we had produced for them for 14 years at that time, but we had to slowly phase it out and replace it with a new item. Because business slowed down gradually over two or three years for that model, we needed to find other items that might suit Motorola. Our key sales manager, Joe White, who had been with the company since 2002, slowly developed small new items such as adaptors and chargers. Finally, the Motorola business slowly returned due to our development of the new model, or we would have been in big trouble.

We developed a successful product for Motorola and contracted with Mean Well, a good manufacturer loyal to DuraComm. Jerry Lin, the founder, had graduated from the same Tatung school system as I did. Tom Zillner, the founder of DuraComm, asked me to help them with power supply sourcing in 1993. DuraComm was one of their first 10 customers. Jerry has high-quality standards, the right strategy, and a great team to help him execute it. As a result, his company has multiple offices worldwide and grew to $1.3 billion in sales in 2023.

Mean Well's strategy is to sell only under its own name, except for a few customers with whom it had worked at the beginning of the company—DuraComm was one of them. However, their business approach is very structured, which sometimes puts us under pressure and makes it difficult to handle their business. Motorola eventually accounted for more than 50 percent of our DuraComm business when I took over in 2011, which can be both good and bad. Eventually we reduced Motorola's share of our business to about 35 oer cent by acquiring new clients and developing new products.

The founder and I divided their shares after two of our shareholders passed away. When I took over in 2011, I also acquired his shares and became the sole owner of DuraComm. Although the company was well-run and profitable, we had to make a few adjustments. One of our leading products, which our engineer John Fuhrman had developed for Motorola several years earlier, was nearing the end of its product cycle. However, they didn't stop purchasing the product immediately but gradually transitioned away from it over several years. We have continued to produce that model for Motorola since 2002. Motorola didn't give us the business for the replacement item because our quotation for their new product was not competitive with another big supplier. Our manager began to develop other items, such as chargers and adapters, and after several years, we recovered some of the lost revenue.

Our problems were that Motorola occupied too big a share of our business, and we, Mean Well, supplied 90 percent of our product line. If they decided not to sell to us, we would need to shut down.

We decided to expand our product line instead of having too many eggs in the same basket. We started a lighting business, which turned out fine, although it was not as successful as I had hoped. Solar energy would be another good product. Although we were able to reduce Motorola's share of our overall business from 50 percent to 30 percent, it still was too much. We were in a niche market where business neither increased nor decreased quickly. I had a small team of employees who created, manufactured, and shipped products rapidly. However, DuraComm has remained a strong, steady company, and Mean Well has thrived.

Nevertheless, adding solar power and LED lighting was not very successful, for reasons I don't understand. I sometimes offered free money to install solar and split the energy savings over 20 years. Kansas City Power and Light (now Evergy) offered an incentive of $2 per watt up to $50,000 and rapid depreciation for the first year. Most of our business was distributed to the East and West Coasts. However, we did several local LED installations in City Hall, Bartle Hall, and Union Station. It is incredibly satisfying when one of my products helps a community organization. Fortunately, DuraComm was considered an essential infrastructure company and could remain open when the city ordered companies to shut down for a few months during the COVID-19 pandemic in 2020. Otherwise, it could have had a big financial impact on the business.

We had a small team of people led by our Chief Engineer Ricardo to create and manufacture products with a short lead time. In other words, if a customer had a specific request regarding their specifications, we could design it and manufacture it here in our Kansas City facility. This was a big advantage for us because the lead time was short compared with shipping from the Far East.

"Benny is a great businessman who has been very successful," Mike Haverty, the previous owner of Kansas City Southern Railway, said. I have been on the board of directors of Union Station Kansas City for 23 years. The job his company did to provide the outdoor lighting to shine upon the Union Station building is amazing. It is only a small part of what Benny's company achieved in doing business in the Kansas City area and worldwide."

Successful entertainers and athletes often stay around too long and regret it. Although I was on top of my game professionally, I began to feel that it may be time to start winding things down and devote more time to my family, community organizations, and hobbies. Around 2007, a company called Vornado, which is based several hours away in Wichita, Kansas, was looking for a way to enter the steamer market. They manufactured products such as fans, heaters, and humidifiers so that steamers would complement their product line nicely.

The leadership decided it would be easier to purchase an existing company rather than start a new steamer division.

Coincidentally, we had adjoining booths at the housewares show in Chicago, and they approached me about selling Top Innovations. I eventually agreed, with one condition. "I don't want to sell the company and have everybody in Kansas City lose their job," I said. "So, you have to stay here for three years."

They agreed, and we closed the deal in 2008. It was the best kind of deal, where everyone came out ahead. I remained a consultant for Vornado for a short time, and because I still owned the building, I collected rent for the next three years. Though they eventually moved the company to Wichita, they still have a small sales office in Kansas City, with many of the same salespeople who worked for me. Shortly after the deal closed, the 2008 housing crisis rocked the economy. "Benny, you are so lucky," my banker said. I agree that the timing was good, although, in business, luck often is the residue of hard work.

After I successfully sold DuraComm to NewMar in 2022, I celebrated with my attorney, accountant, and friends, such as Richard Looney, Jim Poplinger, and their wives, with a nice dinner at the Carriage Club. My accountant told me his records showed I had registered 14 companies. Of course, this means that several of them didn't work out and had to be shut down. However, the victories outnumbered the losses, except for the deal in Barcelona in which I lost $2 million in two years. Fortunately, I was able to address the problem and move on.

Selling not only the DuraComm business itself but also the property was lucrative. Although I never considered myself an expert in real estate, I have been able to purchase attractive properties for both business and personal use when they fit my situation and then sell them for nice profits. I liked to buy small apartments near where I did business, both for convenience and as investments. For example, in 2019, I sold an apartment in Taipei that I had purchased for $1 million for $2 million, which helped compensate for a business loss in Spain.

When I visited Shanghai to open an office in 2000, I bought a 1,000-square-foot apartment for $130,000. This apartment is in a nice area where many Taiwanese, Japanese, and European businesspeople live. It was the first and only place where foreigners could invest in real estate and live in.

One big difference with Chinese real estate is that although you may own the building, you cannot own the land. The land always belongs to the Chinese government. They lend it to you for 70 years, after which time they can take it back, although the government would not ask for the land back unless they needed it for a road or a building.

As I traveled to Shanghai more frequently, in 2008, I hired an interior designer, Mr. Hsieh, to renovate it. I was pleased with the cost and quality of his work. Because I traveled to Shanghai two or three times a year, for one or two weeks at a time, I didn't want to rent it out and risk any damage. I contracted with Mr. Hsieh to clean my apartment every month because it was so inexpensive, and I let him know when I would be coming so it would be clean when I arrived.

One time, when I didn't inform him that I was coming, I walked in and was shocked to see the dinner table littered with beer bottles and dirt. The whole apartment was a mess. I later learned from my security camera and apartment cleaner that Mr. Hsieh often came to my apartment to take a nap or bring a woman with him.

When I told him, he apologized and came to clean my apartment. I told this story to Edith's brother, David, who is good at resolving these types of situations. When David went to talk with Mr. Hsieh, he again asked for forgiveness and even knelt to try to regain my trust, which is not normal for a person to do. I was surprised that some Chinese will do whatever it takes to get business back. For whatever reason, perhaps a lack of family education, he didn't seem to be aware of the importance of treating your client's property as you would your own. Of course, although he seemed genuinely sorry, I never used his services again. The happy ending to this story is that my $130,000 investment eventually grew to a value of more than $1 million, and I sold it in December 2024. In China, there is no annual property tax, and sellers do not have to pay a tax when selling a property. However, in the U.S. when I sold my commercial property, I had to pay a 20% capital gains tax on the profit.

In 2019, I also sold a commercial property I purchased in 2006 in Kansas City to Mean Well for use as its Midwest distribution center. They were originally interested in buying DuraComm, but it was less complicated to purchase the property first.

Although the six-month contract I had signed with a real estate company had expired, I would honor a sales lead if it came from them. The agent asked me to sign a renewal contract that he said would exclude Mean Well from his commission so that if my deal with Mean Well was not successful, he could push another customer to make a deal with me. However, the contract he presented did not include the clause to exclude Mean Well from his commission. Therefore, I refused to sign it.

They brought me a potential buyer who was interested in purchasing our building for $3 million to grow marijuana, which recently had been legalized in Missouri. I told them that Mean Well was interested in buying my building, and I would not have to pay a commission because it was my lead, not theirs. They tried to get me to sign another contract agreeing to pay the commission even if Mean Well were the buyer. I thought they were trying to cheat me, so I had my attorney, Bob Levy, look over the contract and stop it. I was disappointed that the real estate company was so unethical.

Jerry Lin, the owner of Mean Well, owned a warehouse and office in Fremont, Calif., where real estate is about four times more expensive than in Kansas City. After agreeing to negotiate the deal without an agent's commission, he agreed to pay $2.91 million. The agent rushed a new contract to me and urged me to sign it quickly. The realtor was supposed to exclude Mean Well from the contract because Mean Well was my lead, and the realtor would not be entitled to a commission if they bought the property. But the contract didn't exclude Mean Well. Bob Levy saw problems with it and told me not to sign. In the end, it was good to have two sales options, and I believe it set a price record for that part of Kansas City. In business, there is a saying—one buyer is no buyer. You should always find two potential buyers so you can get the highest price possible. Although I have done well in real estate, I have always focused first and foremost on my business, and any profits from the buildings were simply a bonus. As I always said, "I am a businessman—I am not in the real estate business."

Nevertheless, Edith and I still have two properties in Taipei, where there has been a big jump in real estate prices in the last two or three years. We are trying to sell them and convert them into cash, which is easier to use than real estate at our age. If I had spent more time investing in real estate in Taiwan and China, I believe I could have made a lot of money. But, as Edith said, don't be greedy. We were fortunate to earn enough money to live nicely here.

When I was young, a long time ago, before I moved to Kansas City, I read an article by Malcolm Forbes about the benefits of purchasing life insurance tax-free. If we passed away while still owning the company, the IRS could ask our heirs to pay the estate tax on the company, and they would have to sell it quickly, most likely for less than it is worth. Like the Forbes family, when I came to the United States, I purchased irrevocable life insurance to protect my children in case we died. Though I hope we never needed it, I also purchased long-term care insurance to pay for personal care at home.

Shanghai was one of many cities on several continents to which I traveled for business. Although traveling for business can be grueling at times, I always enjoy visiting new places and meeting new people. I try to travel on one airline so I can accumulate points, and I have traveled nearly 2.5 million miles on United Airlines. Although I don't travel as much now that I am retired, I still am a United Airlines Platinum member, which gives me priority boarding privileges. I can also use my airline memberships to upgrade, which is less frequent now or limited to one day before a flight for upgrade confirmation, which does not fit my demands.

Although my travels tend to blur together after so many places and miles, there is one trip I will never forget. Shortly after the terrorist attacks of Sept. 11, 2001, I had scheduled a day trip to Nova Scotia to meet with Barry Ingliss, the general manager of Singer in Canada. The world was still on edge, and security was tight.

As I have mentioned, I have always been interested in world affairs and constantly read about people and events in the news. Because of the events going on in Iraq at that time, I was reading a book about the notorious terrorist Saddam Hussein. The book was written in Mandarin, not English, and Hussein's photo was on the cover.

Although my meeting in Nova Scotia went well, the return trip did not. The problem started when I went through customs in Montreal. Since it was a one-day trip, I had one carry-on bag. Perhaps because I was carrying a new laptop computer, which security said contained a chemical that could trigger security camera alarms, they decided to search my carry-on items. Of course, they saw my book, which was written in a language they didn't understand and with a terrorist's photo on the cover.

To make matters worse, I have a habit of underlining information that I read and jotting down a list of names and page numbers to keep everyone straight. My list of names includes those of many senators, congress men and women, and other politicians. This helps me go back and read about a person again, so I won't forget their details. I also bring a U.S. map to help correctly spell city names. This made the customs officials suspect I might meet the terrorist profile, and they started asking questions.

"My company, Top Innovations, was just named a Top 10 Small Business by the Kansas City Chamber of Commerce," I said. "Will you please call them? Also, I am very close with Representative Sam Graves. Will you please call him?"

They didn't care. I missed my flight, but after checking me out for three or four hours, they finally let me go. I wasn't so much angry as annoyed since it should have been obvious that I was not a terrorist. When I finally got home, I told Sam Graves what had happened. He said, "Right now, we are developing a new fast-check program for frequent travelers." Looking back, I am thankful that this happened in Canada instead of a nation that is not as friendly as the United States. We use the TSA PreCheck program now when we fly.

One of many lessons I learned from Pat Hagerty, a consultant for Singer and other leading appliance companies, is to always travel first class. It is nice to be treated well, especially when traveling internationally. Plus, if an airline changes its schedule, it takes care of its priority customers first. The trade-off, of course, is that first class can be prohibitively expensive.

However, because United Airlines offered a special one-time rate, I took my whole family on a first-class, around-the-world flight. The tickets were a special price for adults and half price for children. Because we were traveling first class, a special concierge from the airline greeted us at each destination and helped us to the next gate or lounge. United Airlines has discontinued this program. Today they offer business class, which is suitable for my needs.

We started our trip in Paraguay, where I had a customer who had purchased one million sandwich makers from Mitco. We visited Adel Rahal, a Singer agent in Paraguay. I had to hire a babysitter to care for Elizabeth and Katherine, who were five and eight years old. We visited Iguazu Falls in Paraguay, where three waterfalls from three countries come together. In Ciudad del Este (which means a town from the Far East) in Paraguay, we visited Jackson Fu, an engineer who had worked as an inspector for Mitco in Taiwan and later moved there and opened a small shop to repair electric appliances. He was a nice person and a good engineer, and he probably left Taiwan too early before the economic boom. Still, he probably did so for political reasons.

After visiting Brazil and Paraguay, we traveled to Spain to visit my customer Jose Grife. He was a smart young man who introduced me to the Spanish market, including the door-to-door sales company Mercedes. He developed a multicooker using a rice cooker with different types of controlling temperatures and times. It became a highly successful item on the market, and I oversaw the sourcing and financing for the product. We shipped more than 100,000 pieces for a special newspaper promotion. I later attempted a joint venture, but it was not successful. However, because of Jose, I began to love Spanish culture and business. Later, I even bought a small, old apartment there in a good location.

However, this led to a disastrous investment in Product Mercedes in 2013, I ended up losing $2 million in 18 months. This was a terrible time in my business career, and shame on me for not stopping my losses quickly enough. To make a long story short, I did not manage my investment well because the general manager and the accounting person he brought with him were neither good nor honest people. It was my mistake that I did not use the original founders who offered to help because of rumors that some employees had filed a lawsuit over my purchase. One hundred people were selling mostly door-to-door, and some even stole the products. This was the darkest time of my business, even though I personally enjoyed the Spanish lifestyle. I had to put this unhappy period behind me and go on with my life.

I have never gambled more than a few dollars for entertainment, although the Chinese will socialize by playing mah-jongg or poker on Chinese New Year. However, I have sometimes gambled in the business world, as in the Spanish company. The difference is that in business, I gamble on myself, and often, I hold the high cards. However, as I am sure Edith would agree, my problem is that sometimes I show my cards too easily.

On the positive side, because of my investment in Spain, Elizabeth also began to love Spain. She studied for her MBA in Barcelona, where all the lectures and textbooks were in

Spanish, and her Spanish is excellent. Unfortunately, she was not able to find a job in Spain after I closed the company. She has lived in Berlin for more than eight years and loves living in Europe. And despite the problems with my business, I still love Spain and was fortunate to have had other business ventures that continued to thrive.

Traveling has introduced my family and me to new cultures and people, and it has given us a greater appreciation of our life in the United States. I have been fortunate to travel to nearly 40 nations:

Australia
Austria
Belgium
Brazil
Canada
China
Cuba
Czechia
Denmark
Egypt
France
Germany
Greece
Hong Kong
Indonesia
Ireland
Israel
Italy
Japan

Jordan
Malaysia
Mexico
Netherlands
Paraguay
Philippines
Portugal
Singapore
South Africa
South Korea
Spain
Switzerland
Taiwan
Thailand
Turkey
United Kingdom
United States

Of course, a serial entrepreneur never completely retires. People knew I had money to invest and were not shy about approaching me. Former Kansas City mayor Charles Wheeler introduced me to a local doctor. He had started a promising business conducting clinical trials for pharmaceutical companies. He needed additional funding to grow the business, and I agreed because I understood its growth potential. I liked investing in a local Kansas City business since I'm well-known here, and my other business ventures were centered on the East and West Coasts. Eventually, I purchased 100 percent of the company and retained him as an employee in what would not turn out to be one of the better deals I have made.

"Benny, you don't know anything about pharmaceuticals," Edith said. "Why are you investing in it?" Several other people said the same thing, and I wish I had followed their advice.

I quickly learned that the doctor's company was sloppily run, which is not good in such a highly regulated industry. What's more, the son of the person from whom I purchased the business was arrested with a minor girl in a police sting and went to jail, so I obviously had to let him go. I replaced him with a doctor from the University of Missouri-Kansas City who understood the clinical research business. One day, he called with the worst possible news.

"Benny, we have a big problem here," he said. "I just learned that our chief nurse used her blood instead of the patient's blood for testing. We advertised for patients, and she couldn't find the type she needed, so she used her own blood."

We immediately fired the nurse, hired an attorney recommended by Bob Levy to conduct a thorough internal investigation, and reported the situation to the U.S. Food and Drug Administration. They sent another lawyer to interview everyone in the company and write a report. The FDA also sent a team to our office to investigate. Because we were proactive and followed the appropriate procedures, their report concluded "no comment," which meant nothing needed to be improved and was the best possible outcome under the circumstances. Because I had been proactive, the Kansas attorney general never had to interview me. Once again, this demonstrated why it is so important to have a good lawyer. However, it soon became clear that the company was finished.

Pfizer, which had been an important client, sent an inquiry about conducting research on a new drug. Their standard questionnaire asked, "Has the FDA ever visited your company? If so, explain why." We responded that they had after we had self-reported the problem and taken care of it. Nevertheless, Pfizer decided it would be too risky to work with us until we strengthened our reputation in two or three years. In the end, I owned the clinic for a little over a year and lost $1million.

It was a tough lesson, but I should have followed Edith's advice about not investing in an industry I didn't fully understand. I'm fortunate that my successes have far outweighed my mistakes over a lifetime in business. A year later, I saw in the newspaper that the Kansas attorney general became involved, sentenced the nurse to jail, and revoked the doctor's medical license. However, they didn't sentence him to prison because of his age. They didn't call me during the investigation because I had already initiated an investigation by my attorney. As Edith always says, "We need to do everything legally."

Even as my business ventures grew, I was also firmly committed to personal growth. I never remain in the same place in life; if we are not moving forward, we are moving back. Fortunately, technology gives us instant access to the most innovative thinkers and writers on any topic, including business.

Nana and Roseline, my secretaries at Midland Taipei and Mitco when I lived in Taiwan, recognized this in me. They both were capable professionals who had majored in English in college. Today, Nana, who later moved to New Zealand, paid me a great compliment, saying that I am able to think logically to analyze the source of a problem and then solve it.

Rosaline mentioned that she was impressed that I continued to purchase and read books after graduating to improve myself continually. To this day, every time I travel to Taiwan, I visit local bookstores to buy books about business, China, Taiwan, and other topics of interest. I once gave a short speech to around 50 people about the economic rise of China, based on the book China Shakes the World by James Kynge.

In our information age, there is no limit to the helpful, fascinating information we can find online. And because books are so inexpensive today, they are a good investment, even if I am able to read only one-tenth of the content. This may be why my bookshelves are so full; I recently counted about a thousand books on my shelves. Because I don't have a great memory, I like to make marks in my books or take notes, especially for people's names. Now that I am retired, I am grateful to have more time to read many books on my shelves, including some I have not touched.

These are a few of the books that have made a lasting impression on me:

Jack Welch and the GE Way by Jack Welch. I met Welch and had my picture taken with him when he visited Kansas City

Execution: The Discipline of Getting Things Done by Larry Bossily

Good to Great by Jim Collins

Awaken the Giant Within by Tony Robbins ·

Charity on Trial by Doug White

People sometimes ask where I see the greatest opportunities for the future and where I would invest my time and money if I were still active in business. Artificial intelligence is the obvious answer. Although, along with most people, I don't fully understand all its potential, AI will have a bigger impact on the world than the introduction of the internet. That impact will happen sooner rather than later. It will revolutionize such fields as medicine. I continue to read and learn as much as I can about AI. I would be tempted to get involved in the industry if I were younger because it undoubtedly represents the future.

Despite being retired, I continue to stay on top of what is happening in the business world. It is in my blood. One of the best things about leaving day-to-day business work is the freedom to pursue a passion I have had since childhood in Taiwan.

Congressman Graves testifying before Congress regarding issues related to non-profit donations

Visited with Czech Republic representatives at the World Trade Center

Duracomm Employee photo

My mother, Edith, and Jenny with my friend, Milo, and his wife at my Taipei apartment

At the Houseware Show in the Top Innovation booth

CHAPTER 7: THE SOUND OF MUSIC

Just like a good movie, my life has a soundtrack. Whether it is classical, jazz, or a completely different musical genre such as Motown, Cuban, or bossa nova, I have enjoyed listening to —and occasionally performing—music for as long as I can remember.

Taiwan has a rich musical heritage that goes back centuries. Although music was taught in our schools, not many people seemed to care because they had other concerns in the years following World War II. I learned more about music from my family and friends, who helped shape my musical tastes than from my formal education.

Few radio stations played popular music at that time as they do today, so my exposure to music mainly came from live performances or recordings. I had a large collection of LP records, which was my passion. Every Sunday, I spent time at the famous Kwang Haw shopping area, where many stores sold LP records. I spent a lot of money on this habit and eventually owned hundreds of LP records.

Although classical music was not widely known in Taiwan, when we were kids my brother owned such records as the William Tell Overture by Rossini and Beethoven's Ninth Symphony, which features the famous Ode to Joy. I quickly came to love classical music and wanted to learn as much about it as I could. I enjoyed inviting friends from school who were interested in music to come to my home to listen to records.

I had a friend who loved music as much as I did. He would often come to my home, and we would not talk much; we would sit and listen to records for hours. He probably was the only friend who shared my habit, but we unfortunately lost contact with each other after we grew up and began work. I knew him from summer music camp; he played the trombone like me. He later worked in the Taipei Symphony as a trombone player and led a jazz band. I want to reconnect with him someday. I also wish I had such a friend now in Kansas City or Taipei. Although sitting down and listening to music for hours rather than talking would be strange, I consider that high-class time.

My uncle, the mayor, helped me find a job at the library after my father died. I met a coworker there who liked music as much as I did. Although he was about 25 and I was only 13, we became good friends. He occasionally took me to his church to listen to classical music, including an annual performance of Handel's Messiah when I was 13. I remember my heart being filled with a feeling I can't describe. In fact, I eventually got baptized in Edith's church after we moved to the United States.

We also had fun learning about music at the library. He was in charge of music activities on Saturday nights, and we would play a classical record on weekends and see if our guests in the library could recognize it. We awarded small prized to those who guessed correctly.

Jazz rivaled classical music for my affection. Another uncle, my father's sister's husband, introduced me to jazz, and I eventually built an extensive record collection. This was unusual because, like classical, jazz was not widely known in Taiwan at that time. I played trombone in the school band and finished second in a competition during summer camp. When our teacher asked us to select an English name, I chose "Benny" because I loved the music of big band leader Benny Goodman. At that time, I didn't realize that I also would start playing clarinet at age 66.

Unfortunately, I didn't know how to play the clarinet at that time. I should have learned to play the clarinet when I chose an instrument at school because your childhood background can change your future. I was told that Benny Goodman decided to play clarinet because, at school, all of the other instruments were chosen by other students. The only instrument left was the clarinet, so he had no other choice. That turned out well for him.

One of the pleasures of moving to Kansas City was discovering that it had a vibrant musical culture in both jazz and classical music. The city was a leader in the emerging jazz age of the 1920s and 1930s, producing such influential musicians as Count Basie and Charlie Parker. The Kansas City Symphony, led at the time by conductor Michael Stern (son of the famous violinist Isaac Stern), plays in the spectacular Kauffman Center for the Performing Arts, which opened after I moved to Kansas City. I am a major contributor to the center's general fund, and Edith and I are recognized with our names on the wall. We also spent a great deal of money on a small, four-seat box that is inscribed with our names—a permanent tribute to our commitment to the performing arts.

Music also thrives in the area's many large and small colleges and universities. Through a series of events, I had the opportunity to play a key role in founding the Park University International Center for Music, which is one of my proudest accomplishments. Park University is a private school in suburban Parkville, Missouri, founded in 1875. Although highly regarded for academics, the center would raise its international reputation. At that time, I was on the advisory board at Park University but not yet a trustee. This was because Charles and Patty Garney had introduced me to university President Beverly Byers-Pevitts.

Like many of my philanthropic adventures, the seeds of the program were planted through a simple introduction. A good friend, Gregory Sandomirsky, a violinist in the Kansas City Symphony, introduced me to the renowned pianist Stanislav Ioudenitch, a Van Cliburn Piano Competition gold medal winner. Stanislav dreamed of starting a music school using the classical European apprenticeship model.

I shared the concept with the university president, and she liked it. He envisioned the music program as eventually serving as an ambassador for the university. When I share an idea that is well received, it usually is time to reach for my checkbook. This time was no exception. I asked Stanislav what he needed to start the program. "First things first," he said. "First, I need a piano. It must be a Steinway made in Hamburg, Germany, not in New York City."

At that time, a good used Hamburg Steinway piano cost about $90,000, so I committed to purchase it. I joked that I would buy one leg a year, so it would take me three years to pay for the entire piano.

Although the president was firmly behind us, not all the trustees were yet on board. To attract the most talented students from around the world, we had to cover 100 percent of their expenses, which were budgeted at $30,000 a year. World-class music students have many good options, so that was the cost of Park University becoming a major player. However, the trustees came around when they saw how the music program put Park University on the international map. A Uzbekistani student named Behzod Abduraimov was the first to become famous. Stanislav recommended him, and he came to Park despite being offered a full scholarship to the Julliard School in New York City.

"No, I'm not going to Julliard, he said. I'm going to Kansas City."

"Are you crazy?" his friends asked.

Behzod came to Park University as a freshman with a full scholarship to study with Stanislav. One year later, at age 19, he competed in the London International Piano Competition and became world champion. He would go on to be very successful, which was great news for the university. He traveled around the world to perform and, at the same time, promoted Park University. When someone asked where he was from, he said, "I am a student at Park University in Kansas City." He could have chosen any place to live but chose Kansas City as his home. Since 2014, he has served as the center's artist in residence. He currently travels about 70 percent of his time. However, he considers Kansas City his home, although he also still has a home in Uzbekistan. So does Stanislav, who bought a house here.

The awards didn't stop there. Kenny Broberg earned a silver medal in the Van Cliburn International Piano Competition. Today, the International Center for Music may be more famous than Park University itself. Stanislav has committed to remaining with the program for the long term, and it currently has about 20 students. More people are donating now because of its success. I am proud that the university president told me I am the only person who has contributed every year since the program was founded. The International Center for Music is transforming talented proteges in piano, violin, viola, and cello into world-class performers. After 20 years, it has become a success story. I appreciate Stanislav's kind words about our friendship.

"*I had the pleasure of meeting Benny Lee at Park University, introduced to me by Park's former president, Beverley Bayers-Pevitts. At the time, Benny was serving as a trustee for the university, and that's when our friendship began. Benny is truly a visionary. He not only pursues his own dreams with passion but also embraces and supports the dreams of others. His belief in the program I founded at Park University, the International Center for Music -- has been unwavering. Benny's deep love for music and his appreciation for excellence have made him a loyal friend and supporter since day one. His dedication to bringing world-class music to the forefront is*

evident. One of the pivotal moments for us was when, thanks to Benny's generosity, we acquired a magnificent Hamburg Steinway for ICM is a testament to his commitment to music and the program's future. Benny's passion for music led him to take up the clarinet, where he showed remarkable dedication! I vividly remember him proudly sharing that, after just a few months of practice, he had learned over 200 songs and could remember every one of them. What an incredible talent!
If ICM had a clarinet program, I would absolutely offer him a scholarship! (Haha!) I hope readers understand Benny's incredible generosity, passion, and ability to bring people together around his love for music, philanthropy, and vision. Benny is not just a successful businessman but someone whose heart has touched the lives of many through his charitable work and his belief in the power of art and education. He has left an indelible mark on everyone fortunate enough to know him."

Although the International Center for Music may be my most rewarding experience, I also support several other instrumental and vocal groups through donations and as a volunteer. These include the Spire Chamber Ensemble and Baroque Orchestra, the Kansas City Youth Symphony, the Kansas City Jazz Orchestra, and Cubanisms, which promote Cuban music and culture.

Elizabeth Lane of Bach Aria Soloists is my neighbor. She surprised me once by coming to my home with her son, a self-trained jazz pianist. We had a great time playing together. I was impressed at how many jazz and popular songs Elizabeth knows. She also did some improvisation, which is unusual for classical musicians, who usually prefer following sheet music.

Another way Edith and I contribute is by hosting fund-raising performances in our home. Although I hate to ask people for money, this also is a good way to enjoy beautiful music in an informal setting. This is one of the great joys of my life because I can spend time with many friends with the same interests as me—eating, drinking, chatting, and enjoying good music. We started doing this when we lived in Briarcliff. We invited Alberto Bologni from Italy, a violinist who is a good friend of Gregory Sandomirsky and teaches music in Kansas City. I paid for his first trip to the United States and have a great time visiting him whenever I travel to Italy. We have become very close friends.

The tradition continued when we moved to our current home at 6300 Ward Parkway. This famous street begins near the Country Club Plaza and travels south near the Missouri and Kansas state lines. Ward Parkway has a wide, landscaped median decorated with fountains and statues. It is home to many of Kansas City's finest houses.

Our house, which was built in 1955, also was really nice—at least until we began to remodel it. Two young women architects had recently graduated from architectural school, had been overseeing the renovation of my office building, and had done a good job, so I hired them to work on our home. Although their original quote for the renovation was $600,000, I eventually ended up spending more than $2 million because I made many modifications and expanded the spaces. I depended too much on the architects to manage the costs, and they didn't do a good job. The cost overruns soon became obvious. The construction crew once wanted to charge $1,200 to install a door. "Why does this cost $1,200?" Edith asked me, and I didn't have a good answer because I was traveling a lot and did not see the details. Edith asked them to take the door down and reinstall it so she could watch to see why they charged so much. They never responded to her challenge.

Finally, the construction foreman called and told my wife, "Edith, my boss cheated you." Instead of a single, all-inclusive bid, they charged for how much time and material was needed. The foreman told me that as many as 10 workers came and checked in each morning, but then many left. "I cannot do that," he said. They had given me an estimate for both material and labor but charged even though their workers were not there.

I responded by contacting several lawyers. One of them said, "Mr. Lee, forget about this. You are wasting your time and money." In a nice way, I told him, "I have time. I just sold my company and have money because I just sold Top Innovations." Although he still didn't take the case, I found another lawyer who was willing to pursue a lawsuit. It took almost two or three years, and I spent more than $700,000. My wife complained every month when I got their invoices for $10,000 or $20,000 for almost two years. Finally, the other party made an offer a few days before the court hearing. Although I wanted to continue the lawsuit as a matter of principle, my attorney finally convinced me to settle for $650,000. Even though he thought I had a 99 percent likelihood of winning, I would be running a risk if the jury disagreed. Fortunately, the contractor's insurance company settled the claim. Even if I won the lawsuit, I would have gotten nothing if they had declared bankruptcy.

More importantly, I was able to hold the contractor accountable for fraud. Although 99 percent of the companies I do business with are highly ethical, this is not the case in the construction industry. where there is so much fraud. I had to pay about another $300,000 to another general contractor to finish everything. Even though I had the financial resources to undo the damage, it was an expensive lesson. If someone is in the construction business and has a good reputation, they can make a lot of money.

I put that experience behind me as we enjoyed entertaining as many as 100 or even 150 guests at our events. One time, we even had more than 275 people for an Alzheimer's fundraiser, which was too many, especially because we also served a light dinner. However, after one of our first parties, Edith told me, "Be careful because so many people are in the great room." After consulting with my architect, we determined that we already had steel beams, so there were no safety issues.

Now, our guests can enjoy good music and even dance with no safety concerns. Despite the hassles, Edith and I do have a great home. We expanded the kitchen and great room and added soundproof materials. It has good acoustics for musical performances and offers a completely different atmosphere from a large concert hall.

One time, we entertained 186 guests who were benefactors of the Kansas City Symphony. They understood that Edith did the cooking and serving with the help of Richard and Sue Looney, and they asked that she not cook so she could enjoy the event as a host. Instead, we paid a little more than $8,000 to hire a caterer whose food was like what Edith served. Although we did so occasionally, she couldn't see wasting money like that.

Edith is an excellent hostess, although now we often have events catered to save her the hard work of cooking and serving. Surprisingly, her mother did all of the cooking when she was a student, so she didn't learn to cook herself until she married me, but she is a fast learner. People always ask how we are able to feed so many people during
events in our home. Richard Looney and his wife, Sue, always help. Richard was my boss when I worked for Midland International, and we remain close friends to this day.

I have a hard time remembering names, especially when I meet so many people in the business world and at events in our home. Someone in the TECO office gave me good advice. He said he spends one day a week reviewing the business cards they have collected and making some type of mark, such as glasses or a bald head, to help connect the name with the person. He had to review them seven times before he could remember them. I am sure that would work well, although I still have problems. I once read that if you can remember the names of people you meet, you will be 50 percent successful. By that standard, I am a 50 percent failure.

We once enjoyed dinner with the former conductor of the Kansas City Symphony, Michael Stern. The documentary From Mao to Mozart is about how his father, the famous violinist Isaac Stern, traveled to China to perform in the late 1970s. While there, he discovered a young cellist named Jian Wang, who later became famous and was scheduled to perform in Kansas City. Shirley Helzberg, a civic leader, knew that I loved music and spoke Chinese, so she invited me to join them for dinner. It was an evening I will never forget.

Julia Irene Kauffman, daughter of the entrepreneur Ewing Kauffman, is a major benefactor of the arts. I had met her several times and once attended a special dinner at her home. When the Kauffman Center for the Performing Arts was under construction, Jane Chu convinced me to donate funds a few times to purchase a box. My donation included having my name listed on the wall and a small, four-seat box. Although it was a sizable investment, it is good to know that my contribution will help Kansas Citians enjoy classical music long into the future.

Because of my friendship with Jane, I saw the model for the center and visited the site during construction. Several times when friends visited, Jo Keatley arranged special visits when no one else was there. Jan Kraybill, the symphony's organist and organ conservator, even showed us the impressive Casavant organ high above the symphony hall. I once showed it to David Hainsworth, a lighting customer from the United Kingdom, and his engineer, David Horsfield. Much to my surprise, David knew how to play the organ—and play it well. He played that organ whenever he visited.

Individuals or businesses can underwrite symphony concerts for a donation of $10,000. Sponsors are announced before the concert, and afterward, they have the opportunity to enjoy a late dinner with the featured performer and several symphony musicians. I have sponsored several concerts, including one by Anthony McGill, the principal clarinetist of the New York Philharmonic. I also had the honor of meeting cellist Yo-Yo Ma and getting a photo with him, Edith, and Elizabeth backstage when he came to Kansas City.

Living in Kansas City has enabled me to enjoy listening to wonderful music of all types and meeting some of the best performers and conductors in the world. Tickets might be much harder to come by in a larger city such as New York. However, since playing trombone in school and guitar in the military, I have not had the time or opportunity to play an instrument other than keyboards.

That unexpectedly changed around Christmas in 2013 when we held an FBI Citizens Academy party in our home. I invited a violinist and two Taiwanese cello and viola players, including Gregory Sandomirsky and Chai-Fei Lin, who were part of a string quartet, to perform. Tzuying Huang, a clarinetist for the Kansas City Symphony, joined the group after her symphony rehearsal. They played the Mozart clarinet quintet K581. It was beautiful, just as you would expect from professionals. Although musicians frequently perform in my home, it was rare to have a clarinetist. Her music was beautiful, and I was captivated. Because the musicians refused to let me pay them for their performance, I invited her back for another dinner of Taiwanese noodles, which is my wife's specialty.

"Am I too old to learn to play the clarinet?" I asked.

"No," she replied.

"Good, I said. Let's start next week."

And that is just what I did. Remarkably, I made a sound during my first lesson, which impressed her. The next week, she taught me the higher registers, so after two lessons, I learned enough of a range of notes to play several songs. Because I knew "Strangers on the Shore" by clarinetist Acker Bilk, I used my keyboard to play the accompaniment because I had the chords stored in my memory. I can automatically play the keyboard accompaniment, although, at that time, I had not learned that I could purchase accompaniment background music. My wife was really shocked. "Wow, is that you?" she asked.

Two weeks later, we held a reception in our home for the Czech and Slovakian ambassadors, so I invited Daniel Veis, a Czech music professor from Park University, to play classical music. During networking time, after several drinks, I played "Stranger on the Shore" on my clarinet and told them I only had two lessons. Peter Gandalovic, the Czech ambassador, said, "I cannot believe it." That certainly boosted my confidence.

Several years later, I played the same song for him during an event in my office to discuss investment opportunities in the Czech Republic. Many Czechs and other high-profile people attended. Although I was impressed by my own skill at the time, I am disappointed that my ability has not advanced much further than a decade later. Nevertheless, I continue to practice, although not as hard as I should.

My friend Mike Haverty attended one of my early performances.

"One of the things that I most remember is Benny playing the clarinet after one of the performances at his home," he said. "Marlys and I told him that he did an outstanding job. He said that he was just in the early stages of learning to play the clarinet. Marlys told him that he was so naturally good at playing the clarinet that he should continue practicing and that he would get even better. He has told Marlys many times over the years that her encouragement that evening prompted him to keep playing and improving. He certainly is now a very talented clarinet player."

I continued taking lessons for a few more months and improving my skills. Unfortunately, my teacher's contract with the symphony ended, and she found an even better job playing bass clarinet for the St. Louis Symphony. But she left a solid foundation, and because I slowly learned to read music, I continued to learn on my own. At that time, I was traveling around 200,000 miles a year, so taking regular lessons would have been difficult anyway.

Although I do not rival my idol, Benny Goodman, I continue to play for my own enjoyment and have even been invited to play in public several times. One of the most intimidating—but rewarding—was playing for Michael Stern and Frank Byrne, who, at that time, was executive director of the symphony. After I had been playing for about three months, I asked Michael to listen to me play when he said he wanted to see me. After I played four songs (50s music, not classical), he gave me some good advice. He recommended spending half of my time working on basics, such as scales or long tones, and half of my time playing songs for fun, as I had just done for him. However, I find myself playing for fun 95 percent of the time while spending only five percent working on basics.

Many of my interests converged when my friend Bambi Shen asked me to help launch a new book she had written called The Uncrushable Rose: A Memoir from Concentration Camp to Being a Free Woman. Bambi is from a prominent family in China, and her ancestor, Shen Baozhen, was a famous official during the Qing Dynasty. Her cousin, Shen Liu-shun, was a Chinese diplomat who had served as a representative to the United States.

Bambi had heard that I played the clarinet, so she asked me to play four songs—two before and two after—her discussion of the book at the Central Branch of the Kansas City Public Library. This was in August 2013, just four months after I had started taking lessons. When Executive Director Henry Fortunato introduced me, he joked, "Our library programs are just like Forrest Gump. You don't know what you can expect or which type of chocolate you will choose. Our good friend Benny Lee would like to present a few songs before and after the book discussion. Benny just learned how to play the clarinet a few months ago." Henry was a special person who once walked 240 miles from Kansas City to Wichita and, later, across Kansas to the Mountain Time Zone. Henry once visited Taiwan with his son. I took care of them for the whole trip, including visiting one of my friends, Milo Tseng, in Tainan in south Taiwan, which has many historic spots. Milo took good care of us and even invited us for a nice dinner and sightseeing.

The 200 or so people in attendance sat down, thinking it might be interesting to see how a beginner played clarinet after four months as they waited for the book presentation. However, after I had played for about 10 seconds, they began to smile. They were surprised at how well I played after such a short time, and they enjoyed it. Seeing them smile and clap made me feel good. I really enjoyed this performance and had a lot of fun entertaining the audience. My friend Bob Levy was one of the people in the audience.

"*When Benny first took up the clarinet, he gave a performance at the Kansas City Public Library following a book talk by an author who was one of his friends,*" *he said. Over the years, I attended many of Benny's performances as they got better and better. I was proud that I could tell him that he did wonderfully at his first concert at the library, while the truth was somewhat less than that.*"

In 2014, after giving a speech, I played for 800 alumni of the Eada Business School at the Art Hotel in Barcelona. When Bambi passed away in 2015, I was asked to play "How Great Thou Art" at her funeral service at Unity Temple on the Country Club Plaza. I considered it to be a great honor.

More recently, I played the Park University alma mater during its 2024 spring commencement, with 5,000 people in attendance. Frank Byrne has mentioned my love for both music and education:

"Benny has a personal love for music, and over the years, he has sought out ways to use philanthropy to bring the power of music to others. He paid for violins to be made for several elementary school children. He has given generously to the Kauffman Center for the Performing Arts to help make this performing arts center a success for our community. His unwavering commitment to make our community a better place to live serves as a shining example to which we all may aspire."

Elizabeth Lane recently asked me to play a piece at the Bach Aria gala, which I enjoyed. Everyone in the audience was a music lover, including the CEO of the Kauffman Center. So many people in Kansas City know that I love to play the clarinet.

In 2019, I participated in the Cremona summer music camp in Italy. Most participants were pianists or violinists, with only about five clarinet players, including a bass clarinet. Although I was one of the oldest and least experienced, I had an opportunity to play the second movement of Mozart's Kegelstat clarinet trio on stage. Despite making a few minor mistakes, I finished the piece and really enjoyed it.

I went again in 2022 because I really enjoyed it. For me, it was a summer vacation—learning and having fun for three weeks. After that, I stayed longer to visit my friend and even stayed in Lucca for three weeks to learn the clarinet from a private teacher, Remo Pieri, a clarinetist from the Lucca Conservatory who teaches at the Lucca Music Institute of Boccherini. He invited me to see the Puccini opera *Turandot* at outdoor theater with a capacity for 4000 people. This was first time I had experienced an outdoor opera performance.

Selling my Shanghai apartment for $1 million helped me buy a nice Steinway piano, model D 274 Spirio, as well as a Mercedes S580. Although Edith is always a very conservative person, because we have enough money to live comfortably, we should enjoy life. For me, music is an important part of my life. Although I don't know how to play the piano, I have enough knowledge of music and understand basic chords. I have been watching many music teaching videos online, and it excites me as I feel I can do it with hard work. I am not talking about complicated classical music, but I believe after hard work, I should be able to play comfortably and enjoy it. This would be the dream of my life. I've set a 10-year goal for myself to hold my own piano concert. That should give me enough time to master the instrument.

I purchased one of the most expensive Steinway models with a recording function. Even though I do not play it, it can play itself. Steinway has rich music software with thousands of recordings of many famous pianists. I can play back exactly what the professional pianists play, with a video showing exactly the keys they play. Although it cost $260,000, it is not crazy for me. My daughter Katherine told Edith, "If Daddy loves it, you should let him enjoy it." The dealer said I probably am the only person in Kansas City with this model, which people rarely buy for use in their homes.

Learning the piano should keep me busy, along with playing clarinet. I have attended Cremona music camp in

Italy twice for clarinet, but now I would like to go for piano. I know it is hard for a beginner like me, but it is my dream.

On March 6, 2025, I hosted a music event at my home to promote the Spire Chamber Ensemble and showcase my new piano. It was a successful event. We had a full house of 120 attendees, good music, good food, good guests, and good networking. I believe my home music concert was one of the best home concerts in the Kansas City area. Former Mayor Sly James was there, as was Jonathan Kemper and his wife and many others.

Having unique home concerts where I can perform, share my upscale Steinway piano, and socialize with my many friends was always one of my dreams. Now, Edith and I are hosting music events almost monthly because everyone we invite loves these unique events.

Here are two samples of the many thank you notes we receive:

"Thank you for such a delightful evening. Benny and Edith, you are the perfect hosts. You make your home so welcoming, and your musical programs are always first class. Thank you for your friendship and for sharing your Steinway with us. "Saludos", Joe and Gloria Bessenbacher"

"Benny, I, too, want to thank you and Edith for a memorable evening. What a piano!! Dr. Chen and the others really did it justice with their beautiful playing. I so enjoyed listening to all the music.

And it was such an eclectic group of people. Alex Shum was Mike's and my violin teacher for twenty years, and I hadn't seen him for a while. Like you, Mike and I started learning a new instrument as adults - I was 40 and Mike was 42.

We sat at dinner with Alan, your biographer. I look forward to reading your biography when it comes out (though he said there continues to be more and more to write about!)

Many thanks again, Linda"

I have been blessed with a lifetime filled with the sound of music. In fact, besides my family and friends, nothing gives me more pleasure.

Violinist Greg Sandomirsky and jazz pianist Bram Wijnands playing at my home event

Food prepared by Edith and Sue Looney saved us a lot of money for catering

The first time I played my clarinet at a party I played Stranger on the Shore, which I learned a few months earlier.

House concert at Briarcliff home with Mayor Duun, Judge Serra, Hon. Slovakia Counsel Ross Marine, TECO Director General

Dinner with cellist Jian Wang at River Club hosted by Helzberg. He was in the movie, From Mao to Mozart, as a kid.

2025 Lee Home Concert Hall - We can host 120 featuring Steinway D Spirio - a favorable venue for professional musicians

CHAPTER 8: FRIENDS AND FAMILY

I enjoy playing the clarinet, whether in public or for enjoyment. However, playing solo is much different than performing in a symphony orchestra, where dozens of musicians blend their skills to produce a sound much more than the sum of the part.

Life also is like that. I am proud of all that I have been able to accomplish business and philanthropy, first in Taiwan and then in the United States. But I also realize that my talents and determination can take me only so far. I would not have succeeded without the countless family members, friends, mentors, business associates, and customers who touched my life in many ways. Like a symphony, life is better together.

My wife, Edith, has been my faithful partner in marriage and business. She always provides sound advice, even when I do not want to hear it. I could have saved myself a lot of headaches (not to mention money) if I had listened to her about several investments. I made a bad investment in Spain, although it provided my family with a deeper understanding of European culture.

Because of my involvement in Spain, my daughter Elizabeth earned an MBA from a business school in Barcelona. Because she has a flair for languages, she opted for

Spanish-language lectures and books. Thanks to her hard work, she now speaks Spanish fluently.

Edith is also very smart and, unlike me, has an excellent memory. She majored in business documentary management in college, which helps explain her amazing organizational skills. When trying to find something I have misplaced, she might say, "Go to my second drawer, open the second page, and you will find what you are looking for." I envy that skill, especially when trying to organize my paperwork. Organization is a skill that I value highly and wish I were better at.

Edith is grounded in her Christian faith and committed to reading the Bible and attending church. I do not doubt that God listens to her and answers her prayers. Although I had always dreamed of moving to the United States, that was not necessarily her goal. I am grateful that she agreed to join me in this great adventure. It has not always been easy as she had to adjust to different customs and learn basic things like driving a car. Although she is not outgoing by nature, she enjoys cooking and conversing with people, which has been a big help with all of the fundraising and entertaining we do in our home.

I am happy that even my friends, such as Mike Haverty, recognize how important Edith has been to my success.

"The friendship with Benny developed many years ago when he invited me and my wife, Marlys, to attend small private concerts that he and Edith would graciously host at their home, he said. *They were relaxing and entertaining. The*

entertainers played a variety of musical instruments, and they were outstanding. Benny and Edith generously provided food and beverages for all of the guests."

The pianist was Tzu-Yi Chen, who had come to Kansas City to study briefly with Stanislav. When Professor Yi Yang Chen came to teach at the University of Kansas, where he is now a tenured professor, she introduced us and told him, "You need to know Benny." I held a small party for Tzu-Yiu's concert. She played *Pictures at an Exhibition*, and I changed pictures in sync with the piano theme. I was learning to play the clarinet then, and that evening, Michael Haverty's wife, Marlys, shared some encouraging words that gave me confidence. In 2024, I traveled to Taipei for Tzu-Yi's wedding.

Bob Levy made similar remarks.

"*One of Benny's great strengths is his relationship with Edith, personally and in business, he said. Their unique combination of Benny's strategic vision and overall approach to business in concert with Edith's attention to detail and focus has contributed to their success in business and life."*

We also are proud of Edith's brother, Leon. After studying chemistry, he also moved to the United States and lived with us at first. He was fortunate to marry Dr. Fan Liu, a wise woman from China who worked as a GPS expert for Honeywell. She later began working for the Federal Aviation Administration near Kansas City International Airport. It was the ideal job because it had good benefits. Leon and Fan have four kids—Jacqueline, Isabella, Caroline, and Allen. Leon earned a degree in chemistry from Tamkang University in Taiwan. When he came to the US he studied computer science at the University of Missouri-Kansas City (UMKC). Then he worked as a bookkeeper for us at Top Innovations and DuraComm. It was a waste of his education because he didn't use what he learned in school. However, his education and ability to take over my office administration and accounting demonstrated that he was smart enough to learn anything. Leon was a big help to our business, and we trusted him implicitly. He is a naturally talented golfer who once shot a hole-in-one. Edith and I love having such close family near us in Kansas City.

I have been blessed with three wonderful daughters. Jenny, my daughter from my first marriage, lives in Los Angeles. I supported her and paid for her education in art school. She is a talented artist who works in the design industry.

Elizabeth Jorden Lee is my first daughter with Edith. Her personality and character are like mine, and she has good language skills. She attended Connecticut College, which had recruited her before graduating high school. After earning a degree in Spanish literature, she studied Chinese for a year in Taipei, which she knew she wouldn't find time to do after starting her career. After studying at Taipei Normal University for one year, she can read, write and speak Chinese. When I had an office in Barcelona, she worked there briefly before enrolling in an MBA program. For the past eight years, she has lived in Berlin, where she is employed in marketing and management. Because of her love of music (which I like to think she inherited from me), she works as a professional DJ a few evenings a week in local coffee shops.

Katherine Berlindar Lee, born three years after Elizabeth, is more like Edith. She has had a successful career as a senior artist in the newspaper business, starting with the *Boston Globe* before moving on to the *Washington Post* and now *The New York Times.* At the *Washington Post,* she was in charge of a project called "Mueller Report Illustrated," which won many awards. Rest of the World, a non-profit organization run by the daughter of Google's owner, Eric Schmidt, selected her as a finalist for its best designer award, even after she had left the company.

Katherine is bright and calm like Edith and doesn't jump into things too quickly. I am proud of her for reaching her longtime goal of working for *The New York Times,* where she's a senior artistic designer in the puzzle department. At age 30, she purchased a 1,000-square-foot flat worth $1 million in Brooklyn. You can see more of her accomplishments at www.katheineblee.com.

We wanted to give our daughters every opportunity to live successful lives, which is the Taiwanese and Chinese way. This includes giving them the best education possible, so we decided to pay for their schooling through a master's or doctoral program. Many Americans, even the wealthy, have a different attitude. They want their children to find their own way and work part-time while in college so they can learn to be independent, which I can understand. However, we believed they should concentrate on their studies, and we were fortunate to have the resources to pay their expenses.

Today, they realize what we did for them and are appreciative. We were pleased when Elizabeth once called to say that she now realizes that many of her friends had to repay student loans, but she didn't. Although private school education was expensive, I am happy that my daughters understood its importance after they grew up.

When our daughters were young and lived in Northland, we decided to enroll them in Pembroke Hill School, which is generally considered the best private school in Kansas City. At first, Edith, who is financially conservative, said, "We don't need to send our kids to an expensive school."

"It's important," I replied. "If our kids are in that environment, they will improve." I believe that, whenever possible, we should give the best to our kids.

Edith broke the news to our daughters that they would be changing schools. Katherine, who had made a close friend in her current school, said, "No, I don't want to go." So, Edith made up a story about why they were transferring to Pembroke Hill. "Unfortunately, your school in our area is full," she told her. "It's occupied. There is no position."

As a kid, Katherine believed it. One day, she told her friend, "I'm sorry, but my parents said I have to leave because there is no position for me." Her friend told her mother, and she said, "No, that's not true. They have more money and want to go to a good school." We still laugh at that story today.

On a more serious note, Elizabeth was in a serious accident on October 9, 2003. A car struck her as she was crossing the street from State Line Road to Pembroke Hill. This was a shock to both Edith and me, and I vividly remember the tears streaming down her face as we rushed to Children's Mercy Hospital. Her face was bloody, and she lost several teeth.

I am pleased to say that things turned out as well as could be expected in the end. Our attorney, Rusty Ruffel, handled the case well; coincidentally, the driver was a longtime friend of his parents. A fund was established to take care of Elizabeth's future needs. I was also impressed when both the head of the school and Representative Sam Graves took the time to visit her in the hospital. I consider us fortunate because things could have been much worse. I have found that Americans often tend to step out in traffic and assume cars will stop, but the rule of thumb to stop, listen, and look both ways is excellent advice.

I am so lucky that I had a classmate, Ken Yang, who studied electrical engineering and came to the United States to get his master's degree. After working with Premier (which used to be part of Spring), he went to China to study Chinese medicine and get a degree and license because his father was a Chinese doctor in Taiwan. He has a lot of common sense and learned from his father. He was one of our class's best students and got good grades. He feels it is important to use his knowledge to help people in the community solve problems that regular hospitals cannot, and many of his patients have no medical insurance.

I used to have high blood pressure. One day, our doctor, Chip Leurding, with whom we were very close, told me, 'Mr. Lee, welcome to senior age. You have high blood pressure. But do not worry. Just take a small pill."

"For how long?" I asked.

"For the rest of your life," he replied.

Dr. Yang told me it is not good to take any pill because it might have some side effects. Taking it every day may affect my other organs. So, I started to get acupuncture from him once a week. Amazingly, my high blood pressure was gone. I had acupuncture every week until a few years ago when Dr. Yang moved to New Jersey.

He introduced me to Dr Ren. Ken Yang's daughter, Sharon Yang, is the managing director and global head of regulatory affairs at JP Morgan Chase. She previously was deputy assistant secretary at the U.S. Treasury Department.

Gregory told me he found a perfect masseuse, Amy Gao, in Dr. Ren's place. I tried it, had very good results, and have been doing massages once a week for over eight years. She could be a doctor because she knows so much about the human body. She learned her skill and knowledge in China from a Chinese medical master who treats patients with traditional Chinese medicine. I am amazed with Chinese medicine and massage, which are based on a thousand years of experience. I was also amazed at how much Amy's medical knowledge. Unfortunately, she does not know much English, otherwise she could be a doctor.

I can feel my health has improved significantly. When I told people that I was going to have acupuncture or massage, they would ask, "What is wrong with your body?" I told them, "Nothing is wrong—I am using acupuncture for preventative care."

I think I am a perfect example of how to take care of your health. (I should not speak too loudly because once you say it,

God could take it away if you are too proud or show off too much.) At age 78, my health is good. I have had no problems after I had a simple operation, so-called Aquablation therapy, a newly introduced technology to treat the prostate. I now have perfect vision after surgery on both my eyes, called PanOptix, to replace the intraocular lens.

I am so lucky to have good health and a good life. With music and a retired life, I do not expect to have dementia or any old man diseases. With learning clarinet and piano, I have a good attitude with my life.

I have been blessed with many strong friendships with business associates, civic leaders, musicians, and more. I also have gotten to know several leading politicians, which is much easier to do in the United States than in Taiwan. Although I was not committed to either political party when I arrived, I did have strong feelings about my new home.

The United States, like every other nation, is not perfect. But moving here only confirmed my longtime belief that it is the best country in the world. Whenever I have an opportunity to speak in a small setting or to a big group, I say many people do not realize how much the United States has contributed to the world. Americans have protected millions of people in the world by safeguarding democracy. I am one of them. If America didn't protect Taiwan 40 or 50 years ago, I would be Chinese today. "If the United States is such a bad country, I ask, then why are they smuggling people here?"

A few years ago, Chinese women came to Los Angeles illegally and gave birth. Their children were considered U.S. citizens, and the government paid for everything. Today, if a

Chinese person wants to come to the United States, they can pay maybe $10,000 to a middleman, get a fake passport, go to Mexico, and walk across the border. Although the journey is dangerous, they feel safe when they arrive in the United States. I think we should be stricter. There is a reason there is a border. This is not fair to immigrants like me who do things the right way.

I realized that my views are more closely aligned with the Republican Party than the Democratic Party, so that is what I became. Soon after I arrived in Kansas City, I visited with Elizabeth Chu, the director general of the Taiwan Economic Cultural Office, who was active in the community.

"Politically, you have to choose Democrat or Republican," she said. "Choose one party—it doesn't matter which one—and get involved."

President Bill Clinton also encouraged citizens to become involved. Someone said we should not get involved in politics, but politics affects us. Dennis Oyer, a good friend and business associate at Midland, happened to be a staunch Republican, and he convinced me to join the party. One thing I learned about the United States is how simple it is to get involved—all you have to do is donate money.

I also made a few political friends, such as my attorney, Terry Kilroy. We traveled together to Washington, D.C., for many political events, including the Republican National Convention. My friend Rick Flaherty, the son of Singer President John Flaherty, once told me he saw me on TV during President George W. Bush's nominating convention.

I began supporting Representative Sam Graves, a Republican who still represents the northern tier of Missouri, while living in Briarcliff. When Elizabeth was in grade school, I took her to Washington, D.C., to learn about our nation's capital. I made an appointment to visit Representative Graves in his office.

"Mr. Lee, what can I do for you?" he asked.

"Nothing," I replied. "I just came here to introduce myself and donate to your campaign."

Judging by his response, this was not something that politicians hear very often. We invited his office staff to Capitol Grille for dinner, and they arranged a tour of Capitol Hill and other important landmarks for us. I told them I am Taiwanese and explained why Taiwan is important to the United States. I am more involved in state and national than local politics. I enjoyed meeting my representatives and discussing issues important to our business community. Former Senator Christopher "Kit" Bond, who also had been governor of Missouri, once visited our home. I didn't think my political donations were that impressive until, in 2002, the *Kansas City Star* ran a story listing the top donors in the area. To my surprise, I was in the top 10 on the list, behind such people as Donald Hall Jr. of Hallmark Cards. I also noticed that Farhad Azima was on the list. He is a billionaire who lives in our neighborhood. I can't compare myself to billionaires because I am just a regular person.

I once joined the National Republican Senatorial Committee, which cost about $5,000 and met quarterly at high-class hotels in different cities. About 70 people typically attended, and various senators would make presentations. They also arranged opportunities to meet and have my photo taken with various senators and other political leaders, and we visited such famous locations as Rockefeller Center. I enjoy these kinds of events.

Other politicians took notice of my interest in politics. When former President George W. Bush visited Kansas City, I donated a few thousand dollars and was able to meet him. I also have met former President Donald Trump, former Vice President Dick Cheney, the late Senator John McCain, and others. As a businessman, it is essential to make your voice heard. But, at the same time, I understand that not everyone shares my views. I always try to separate my personal and professional lives and not discuss politics in the office. Many of my neighbors on Ward Parkway support Democrats, so I avoid conflict by not discussing politics.

When I first moved to Kansas City and started getting involved in politics, Edith gave me some wise advice: Don't become a politician because people will either love you or hate you. Former Mayor Mark Funkhouser once nominated me to be a commissioner of Kansas City SmartPort, which received a lot of media coverage. After I saw several unfavorable comments about me in the newspaper, I followed Tom Zillner's advice by not taking the position. I have been fortunate to meet more people, travel to more places, and enjoy more experiences than I could have imagined while growing up in postwar Taiwan. Knowing my name will be acknowledged in places like AdventHealth Shawnee Mission and the Kauffman Center for the Performing Arts is nice. But it is far more important to me that my family and friends will remember me as someone who always tried to do the right things in the right way.

Because relations between China and the U.S. worsened, the economic situation in China was negatively impacted. Many of my friends have had problems sending money out of China, for example, after they sold a factory. I had an apartment in Shanghai, which I bought in 2002. I was lucky to have David Lee, Edith's brother, help me sell it. He manages Mitco Taiwan for Duracomm and is well-connected. With his help, I sold my 1000-square-foot apartment for over $1 million. I had to pay over $200,000 in capital gains tax to the IRS and the State of Missouri.

Hosted Czech business forum at Duracomm Office

Me and Edith in Brazil - Leandro da Silva arranged for a helicopter to visit companies to avoid traffic congestion.

United Way Tocqueville Society members visiting Taipei United Way

Opposite: Shooting at the FBI Citizen Academy Class in 2008

Park University Trustee - at Student Graduation Ceremony

FBI Citizen Academy Board

July 12, 2018

FBI Director Cris Way visiting Kansas City to meet the FBI Citizen Academy Board members

CHAPTER 9: LEAVING A LEGACY

In his classic leadership book *The 7 Habits of Highly Successful People,* author Stephen Covey recommends beginning with the end in mind. In other words, decide what you would like to accomplish and what you would like others to say about you later in your life, and then work intentionally to make that vision a reality.

I have always known what I would like to achieve: 1) Be known as a devoted husband, father, and friend. 2) Start and grow successful businesses that put my employees and customers first. 3) Not only become an American citizen but actively participate in its democracy. 4) Give my time, talent, and treasure to help improve my community. 5) Take time to enjoy music, travel, and all that life has to offer

Thanks in part to the determination and hard work—and even more to the countless people who have helped along the way—I have realized most of these dreams. However, even after seven decades, I know the future offers more people to help, more things to experience, and more music to enjoy.

Nothing is more important to me than my reputation. Many times, especially when working in China early in my career, it would have been easy to take a bribe under the table or pay off corrupt officials to make things go more smoothly. Nobody would have known … except me.

As I often say, I was never the best student, the most brilliant engineer, or the greatest businessman. But I was able to see a need in the marketplace, connect the dots, and deliver products that made people's lives a little better. All of my suppliers and customers knew that if they worked with me, I would give them the best product at the best price without a hint of dishonesty. My wife Edith studies the Bible and knows more about faith than I do. But if there is one principle I have found to be true, time and again, it is that if you do something good, God will take care of you.

Again, humility is one of my core values. Rather than talk about yourself, it is far better when your friends have good things to say. That way, you know you must have said or done something positive that encouraged them along life's journey. I asked several friends for their thoughts and am grateful and humbled by their remarks.

"I first met Benny in 2013 when I was the district director of the Kansas City district of the U.S. Small Business Administration, as he was well-known as a highly successful entrepreneur and philanthropist. I later worked directly with him when I was the president and CEO of the Command and General Staff College Foundation and he was serving on our foundation's board of trustees. I am proud to be a friend of Benny's. He is a wonderful member of our community. As a business owner, he has been highly successful, contributing to our community's economic well-being and providing jobs, both directly and indirectly, to hundreds of people, and has been a leader at several chambers of commerce, helping others to

succeed. As a supporter of the arts, he has sponsored numerous cultural activities to include musicians and often opens his home as a venue to showcase their talent. As a community leader, he has provided substantial support to a local medical center, several local universities, and civic improvements. As a supporter of veterans, soldiers ,and military families, Benny has funded capital improvements for a VFW post and supported numerous programs of the CGSC Foundation, which directly benefited service members and their families. I will remember Benny as a good friend that I could always count on. He graciously gave of his time as we spent many hours discussing projects and activities, and he always provided helped with anything for which I asked. Benny is a man who should be remembered—and emulated—as someone who succeeded at the American Dream and used his wealth to do good."
-- Roderick M. Cox, Colonel, US Army (Ret.)

"Our relationship evolved step by step, from business partners to close friends. Benny's journey has been truly remarkable. His dedication, foresight, and generosity have left a lasting impression on everyone who knows him. I remember when Benny sponsored a volunteer couples' trip to Taipei. Another memorable occasion was a charity banquet in Fremont, Calif., where Benny delivered a powerful speech on `One Supplier, One Wife' and played the clarinet, leaving everyone deeply touched. Benny has lived a vibrant and remarkable life. As a young man, he achieved great success in integrating and leading businesses across the United States, China, and Taiwan. In his middle years, he passionately dedicated himself to philanthropy

and music. Now, in his later years, he has embraced a life of elegance and refinement. Benny's life is an inspiring testament to success, generosity, and elegance."
-- Jerry Lin, Owner of Mean Well

"My overall thoughts about Benny begin with his integrity, sense of purpose, and dedication to his businesses, his employees, his family, and his friends. The phrase `his word is his bond' is probably overused, but it is particularly applicable to Benny. In business, we dealt with literally hundreds of issues and people over the years, and never did Benny vary from his strong sense of what was right and wrong or shirk his responsibilities. As a friend, he is always supportive of those to whom he is close, going beyond the call of duty. We shared the experiences of our families through ups and downs, and he always put his family first and met their needs.

We were negotiating the sale of one of Benny's businesses when the negotiations became very complicated and disjointed. The other side made an accusation that Benny and I were not acting in good faith. Regardless of the consequences, Benny terminated the negotiations at that point. That was not something that he would tolerate as a man of integrity, creativity, and principles. It's easy to be a good guy when things are going well. Obviously, over the decades, there were things that didn't go so well, but Benny never took the easy way out and always stayed true to his principles. His devotion to and knowledge of Taiwan and its circumstances is encyclopedic. I have learned more from him on that important subject than I can express."

-- Bob Levy, Attorney

"I think that Benny should be recognized as an outstanding entrepreneur who came to this country and achieved great business success, adapted to U.S. policies, and ended up living the American Dream in Kansas City, an area with Midwestern values on both sides of the state line in Missouri and Kansas, and a very philanthropic metropolitan community. Benny and Edith fit right in with the community, and Marlys and I are proud to know them both."
-- Mike Haverty, Kansas City Southern (retired)

"Benny Lee is a leader who combines business acumen with deep philanthropic commitment. He has a keen sense of anticipating future trends in business while addressing current needs. His forward-thinking approach and creative solutions are his assets for his business success. Nevertheless, his business success aside, he is better known in the Kansas City area for his philanthropic support for the community. His generosity extends across education, the arts, business, and many other fields. He is someone who understands that his purpose is to serve others. More than anything else, Benny is a devoted friend who genuinely supports and values others' passions and endeavors. Benny once shared, 'What is money worth if you are not going to put it to good use?' He truly embodies this belief by dedicating his time and resources to giving back to his community. I hope people remember Benny as a visionary businessman whose success was not just about personal gain but about creating a lasting impact through

philanthropy an community service. His legacy is built on a genuine commitment to making a difference."
-- Sook Park, Executive Director, Asian American of Commerce of
Kansas City

"First and foremost, Benny is an amazing human being. His commitment to his family, community, and partners is paramount. Benny is a kind, thoughtful person. Over time, we became much more than acquaintances. We became good friends. Benny is extremely generous with his philanthropy. From his support of the International Center of Music at Park University to his support of the KC Chamber of Commerce and the United Way, Benny was always there when his community needed him. Benny is an extremely creative businessman. Benny looks at problems as opportunities. He is willing to take risks that many others would shy away from. He is an entrepreneur at heart, always trying to solve complex problems to make the world a better and more interesting place. I have great respect for what he has accomplished, especially in the United States, which was his adopted country. I hope people will remember his kindness and his willingness to explore new ideas and opportunities. He has enriched my world. I know that he has done the same to countless others."
-- Peter DeSilva, Banker

"Benny is an outstanding member of the Taiwanese community. We not only were business associates but also became good friends. One time, I told him that now that he was

in the United States, he needed to focus more on the community. He asked me how to start. I said it's not too difficult and that he should make contact with American politicians. One day, he told me he had received an invitation from the White House. I said, 'You will have an opportunity to meet with President Bush. Tell him to support Taiwan.' When Benny came back, he said, 'I met with President Bush and told him what you told me to.' I asked him how President Bush responded, and he said the President told him, 'It's the easiest thing to do.' I couldn't think of anything to say about Benny that isn't good. Benny is everything—generous, social, sincere, and helpful to people in need."

-- Elizabeth Chu, Former Taiwanese consul

"Having met Benny Lee was an absolute enrichment in my life. When we, the Hannover Committee, hosted a 16-member jazz band from Hannover, Germany, for diverse jazz concerts and workshops in Kansas City, Benny and his wife, Edith, invited the band and 100 guests to their beautiful and spacious home for a special reception where musicians and audience could mingle and get to know each other. I will be forever grateful for Benny's generosity. Benny does these receptions for many groups. Benny is just interested in many aspects of life and many cultures. This keeps him so active, alive, and open. He is such an inspiration to others. I wish we had more Benny Lees; the world would be a better place. I also admire his drive in studying the clarinet. He has become very good at it. I call him a musician. Music is very dear to me. I have a fond memory of when Benny and Edith visited

our home at Christmas to experience the German Christmas tree with real candles. The evening ended with a `hauskonzert,' with Benny playing his clarinet, my daughter Kristina the flute, and my granddaughter Rebecca her alto clarinet. It was beautiful and such a joy. Benny's generosity stands out, and so does his interest and involvement in students' advancements, his support of local orchestras and symphonies. classical and jazz, and international cultural exchanges...I could go on and on. I feel honored that Benny Lee is my friend."

Dr. Traute Kohler, Chair of the Hannover Committee of
Sister City Association of Kansas City

Do not look for my legacy in the awards I received, the plaques commemorating my donations, or the products I have sold. Look for it in my wife, daughters, friends, business associates, and community leaders whose lives have touched mine. If they can say their lives were better because of knowing Benny Lee, I will consider myself a success.

Press release event for me and Edith in the Atrium at the Shawnee Mission Medical Center

The 2014 Philanthropist Award presentation

Press release event for our donation and the naming of the Benny and Edith Lee Atrium in 2014

Edith and me on our wedding day

I used green outdoor lighting on St. Patrick Day. Duracomm Lighting was in this business.

Play Park University 2024 Graduation Ceremony. I played Park Alma Mater for 5,000 people in the audience

2025-3-6 Home Event for Spire Chamber Ensemble - Alyssa Nance Soprano

3/6/25 event with new Steinway Piano and Spire Chamber Ensemble - 120 guests - KU Professor Yi Yang Chen played piano.

New Steinway Piano D Spirio - I enjoy life by listening to performances via Steinway's Spiriocast streaming technology.

CHAPTER 10: THE 3CS: CHANGE, CHALLENGE, AND CHANCE

Thousands of books, articles, and speeches have been written about how to achieve success in business and life. Although I am sure most convey at least part of the truth, success is too big—and much too complicated—a topic to boil down to a simple formula.

I could probably write another book about the keys to success and still barely scratch the surface. But, as I think back, I can summarize my thoughts as what I call the 3 Cs: change, challenge, and chance, which I first read about in a book many years ago. Change always creates challenges, which in turn provide plenty of chances or opportunities—if we recognize and take advantage of them.

Change

"*Here's to the crazy ones. The misfits. The rebels. The troublemakers. The round pegs in the square holes. The ones who see things differently … they change things. They push the human race forward. And while some may see them as the crazy ones, we see genius.*" -- Steve Jobs, founder of Apple

I studied electrical engineering at a time when vacuum tubes, not semiconductors were considered state-of-the-art. When I was introduced to computers and learned to use DB2 for business data management., I could not have imagined that ordinary people one day would hold more computing power in the palm of their hands than was used to land a man on the moon. Change is constant in our world today, and it is picking up more speed each year. It is essential for a successful business or life to anticipate change and prepare to meet it.

Challenge

"*I encourage you to challenge your current mindset and start thinking of each day as an opportunity to crush it, to step out of your comfort zone and go all in on what you truly want. Start building the mindset to fight for what is important.*" -- Tim Tebow, former professional football player

I had built a comfortable life by the time I was in my forties. I am sure that things would have turned out fine if I had stayed in Taiwan and continued my business there. But I dreamed of moving to the United States, competing with the world's leading businesses, and enjoying new adventures. I accepted the challenge against the advice of several people I respect.

Likewise, I would have been happy simply to listen to great music through recordings or live performances. However, my appreciation of music is much greater because I challenged myself to learn to play the clarinet when I was in my sixties. This is an endless, lifelong journey because there are no limits to learning about music. Now that I am retired, I plan to improve my ability continually. I give back by playing my clarinet in church on Sundays.

Chance

"*Take a chance! All life is a chance. The man who goes farthest generally is the one who is willing to do and dare.*" -- Dale Carnegie, motivational speaker and author

Some people are convinced that life is all about random chances, with most of the good or bad things that happen to us being beyond our control. I also believe in chance, but I define it as the moment when preparation meets opportunity. Building a high-quality clothes steamer at an affordable price prepared me for the opportunity to go on QVC and sell 16,000 products in a day.

Although I wrote this book for my family, I hope my friends will also enjoy it. I am proud that I have donated millions of dollars to worthy causes, and I hope others can learn from my example. Some people can do more, and others can do less, but we all can do something to make the world a better place. Kansas City welcomed me and my family with open arms, and I am grateful to say I am not a debtor but a creditor for my community.

At age 78, I am in good health. My acupuncturist, Dr. Yang, and my masseuse, Amy, told me I have very smooth skin. I think this is from my DNA or nature, and it is all controlled by God. I appreciate it. I love God, who gives me everything I have. Thank you!

What are the changes, challenges, and opportunities in your own life? What would you attempt if you had unlimited resources and knew that you could not fail? Dare to dream and become all that you can be. I am proud to have donated millions of dollars to worthy causes.

I hope you enjoyed reading my book. As fun as it has been to look back, I prefer to look forward. There are still new chapters to write, and the best is yet to come. Now, go and write the next chapter of the life you have always wanted to live.

APPENDICES

Appendix A

Awards and Honors

- Honorable Chairs of Spire Chamber Ensemble, 2025
- Co-Chair of The Derby Party by Kansas City Museum, 2025
- Emeritus 2024 Command General Staff Staff College Foundation
- Director emeritus, Asian American Chamber of Commerce of Kansas City, 2021
- Honoree of the KC Shepherd's Center 70 Over 70, 2021
- Honorary chair, Park University International Center of Music (ICM) Inaugural Gala, 2019, Maestro Award
- Southtown Business Achievement Award (DuraComm), 2019
- Park University Torchlighter Award for longstanding contributions to the university, 2017
- American Business Bronze Award for Business Innovation, 2017
- Event chair of Kansas City Jazz Orchestra Gala, 2015
- NPR KC Radio Interview - 2015 Benny Lee On Innovation
- Kansas City Philanthropist of the Year, 2014
- Shawnee Mission Medical Center's new birth center atrium was named for Benny and Edith Lee, 2014

- 2013 certificate of recognition, Kansas City Chinese Association
- U.S. Chamber of Commerce Top 100 Small Businesses, 2013
- *Thinking Bigger Business* magazine cover story, August, 2013
- Greater Kansas City Chamber of Commerce Top Ten Small Business Award, 2013
- *Ingram* People Power Money Report - Ranked #45 89.25% business growth from 2009-2012, June 2013
- Central Midwest finalist for the Ernst & Young Entrepreneur of the Year award, 2012
- *Thinking Bigger Business* Magazine - Cover Story and Hall of Fame Award 2013
- One on One PBS KCPT Interview by Victor Hogstrom
- Named a member of The Honorable Order of Kentucky Colonels
- *KC BUSINESS* Top Ten Award, 2012
- Small Business Administration Minority Small Business Region 7 Champion, 2011
- Ingram's magazine's "50 Missourians You Should Know," 2011
- Kansas City Minority Enterprise Development Committee Manufacturer of the Year, 2011
- Governor's Minority & Small Business Award (Missouri Department of Economic Development), 2011
- Man-of-the-Month Fraternity, 2011
- Entrepreneur-in-Residence, University of Missouri-Kansas City Institute for Entrepreneurship & Innovation
- Finalist: Lewis Shattuck Small Business Advocate Award (National Small Business Association), 2011

- Sister City Association of Kansas City President's Award, 2009
- Kansas City Mayor's Proclamation, Benny and Edith Lee Night, March 26, 2008
- Asian American Chamber of Commerce Civic Leader of the Year, 2007
- 25 under 25 by Small Business Monthly- Top Innovations, 2007
- KCPT public television one-on-one interview by CEO Victor Hogstrom, 2007
- Pinnacle Award, Northland Community Foundation, 2005
- Benny Lee testifies before Congressional Subcommittee supporting lower tax deduction limit for charitable giving, 2006
- Top 10 Small Business - Top Innovations, 2003

Appendix B

Community Leadership

- Board director, Kansas City Museum Foundation
- Board director, Spire Chamber Ensemble
- Former Board director, Kansas City Youth Symphony
- Advisory board member, KSHB-TV, 2021
- Board member, Cleveland University, Kansas City, 2025
- Board Member of MAPAA Mid-America Performing Art Alliance, 2025

- Past advisory board member, Greater Kansas City Council of the Navy League of the United States: USS Kansas City
- Former Board member, Command and General Staff College Foundation, CGSC
- Former board member, Kansas City Jazz Orchestra, 2021 to 2022
- Former board member, American Asian Chamber of Commerce
- Command General Staff College, Emeritus
- Advisory board, Park University International Center for Music (ICM)
- Graduate Student Advisory Board, Kansas State University
- Honorary chair, Park University International Center of Music (ICM) Inaugural Gala, 2019
- Honorary chair, Park University Night at the Helm, 2017
- Formal Business School Advisory Board, University-Missouri Kansas City
- Founding member, Park University Trustee Society
- Former trustee, Park University, June 2002 to June 2011
- Former board member, FBI Citizen Academy
- Former board member, Greater Kansas City Foreign Trade Zone
- Former advisory board member, Mid-America Asian Cultural Association
- Former advisor, Taipei Economic and Cultural Office, Kansas City
- Former board member, Alt Cap (Kansas City, Missouri Community Development)

- Former board member, Greater Kansas City Chamber of Commerce
- Former board member, Greater Kansas City Chamber of Commerce: Small, Diverse, Emerging Business Council
- Former trustee, Truman Medical Center
- Former board member, Southtown Council
- Former board member, International Relations Council

- Former board member, Greater Kansas City United Way
- Vice-chair, Chinese-U.S. Sculpture Garden
- Board member of United Way of Greater Kansas City
- Kansas City Global Commission - appointed by Mayor

Personal Website

https://benny-lee.com

StoryTerrace

Made in the USA
Coppell, TX
05 January 2026

68130148R00138